Mind, the Beggar?

LASTING HAPPINESS IS POSSIBLE

Anandmai

INNER AWAKENING MYSTERIES

Editor: Surbhi Lal
Cover Design: Inner Awakening Mysteries
Cover Illustrations: LogoDesign Team

First Printing, 2015

ISBN 978-0-9965863-0-6

Inner Awakening Mysteries
www.innerawakeningmysteries.org

For my Guru, who guided me to the light and love inside,
with love and gratitude

Contents

CHAPTER ONE

Mind, the Beggar?

Is your mind a beggar? What an interesting thought—could it be? You be the judge after reading this story my Guru told me after I was asked a similar question. This story is about King Nan and a beggar and his begging bowl....

King Nan was a good king. He ruled fairly and did not overtax his people. He spent the tax money improving the infrastructure of his kingdom and creating jobs. He was well liked by his people and his family. But the king was not satisfied, even though his people were happy and he had everything—a beautiful wife, devoted children, a prosperous kingdom and adoring citizens. He thought his kingdom needed to be expanded. He craved a larger kingdom and felt the need to slowly take over the region.

King Nan was renowned for his generosity. It was widely known that the first person to encounter the king when he exited his palace could ask him for anything and it was given. One day as he was leaving his palace for his routine morning walk, he saw a beggar who wore tattered clothes but had a beautiful, jeweled begging bowl in his hand. This had the king perplexed; he went to the beggar with the beautiful bowl and asked, "Why are you begging, when you have such a valuable bowl?"

The beggar replied, "Why does that matter? If you do not wish to give me anything, just say so."

At that King Nan got angry and said, "What do you want?"

The beggar laughed and answered, "You are asking me as though you can fulfill my desire!"

Now the king was offended and his pride bruised, so the king said, "Of course I can fulfill your desire. Did you not notice that I am a king, and can give you anything you need? Tell me, what do you desire?"

At this the beggar warned, "It would be wise for you to think carefully before you promise me anything."

You see, this beggar was no ordinary beggar. He was an enlightened, spiritual being in a beggar's disguise who wanted to teach the king a lesson.

The king declared, "Everyone knows that the first person I encounter on my morning walk is granted anything he or she desires."

The beggar then replied, "It is a very simple desire. You see this begging bowl? Can you fill it with something?"

The king smiled to himself as he thought this to be a very easy request. He instructed one of his ministers to fill the beggar's bowl with gold coins.

The minister began to pour coins into the bowl; however, the coins would merely rattle around in the bowl before disappearing. Astonished, and in an attempt to fulfill the beggar's request, the minister continued to pour gold coins into the bowl. Regardless of the number of coins he poured, they continued to disappear and the beggar's bowl remained empty.

People in the courtyard outside the palace witnessed this marvel, and before long, word spread throughout the kingdom and a crowd gathered around the king and the beggar.

Stunned, the king felt his reputation was at risk if he was unable to fulfill the beggar's request. He would rather lose his entire kingdom than violate his vow to satisfy any wish of the first person he encounters when he exits the palace. The king ordered the minister to bring more riches to fill the beggar's bowl. The minister poured more gold coins, and even diamonds, rubies, emeralds, pearls and other treasures into the beggar's bowl. However, while the king's treasury was rapidly depleting, the bowl remained empty. The begging bowl seemed to be bottomless. Everything that was poured into the bowl immediately vanished. Hours went by and the minister continued his attempt to fill the beggar's bowl and uphold the king's honor. Eventually, it was almost nighttime, and the king remained dumbfounded while the crowd stood in complete silence.

Unable to bear it any longer, the king admitted his defeat and fell to the beggar's feet. The king pleaded with the beggar, and asked, "what is this begging bowl made of?!"

The beggar laughed and replied, "It is symbolic of the human mind. There is no secret. It is simply made up of human desires. You fulfill one desire, and another desire is standing just behind it waiting to be satisfied—like my bowl. You put anything in your mind and it disappears, leaving your mind waiting for more; and you put in more and that too disappears, and your mind begs for more—it is endless, bottomless. We move from one desire to another and our bowl is always empty like a beggar's bowl—and every desire is frustrating until it is fulfilled, and the cycle continues and prevents you from focusing on the emptiness you feel inside."

King Nan understood the truth in the beggar's words and beseeched, "What do I do? How do I break the cycle? How do I fill this emptiness?"

CHAPTER TWO

Introduction

M*ind, the Beggar?* is a book that shares words of wisdom from personal experiences, shows the way to peace and joy, and provides the practical tools to get there. It is possible to achieve peace and master your mind, and it doesn't have to wait a moment longer.

Most of us have an inkling of what peace might feel like and we often daydream about feeling that peace away from all the turmoil of mind and heart. To me, peace is like a steady, calm waterbody with no waves from inside to disturb it.

However, the "how" of achieving this peace and the tools to do so, are often elusive or seemingly complicated and seem impossible to apply while living life. Rather peace seems to be attainable only after retirement or by giving everything up and living a secluded life in the mountains. I'm here to tell you differently.

Before we get started, let me share some details about my own journey.

I have lived what most people would call an interesting life, spanning three continents. I got married to a wonderful man on one continent, and had two incredible children on two different continents. I finished my undergraduate degree on one continent and pursued my graduate degree on another. I then worked for hire, i.e. a corporate job, and we attained the typical American dream of a house with a white picket fence, two kids and two cars. I enjoyed having an active and vibrant social life—from going to a Yanni concert at the Taj Mahal to parasailing in Thailand to bungee jumping in the U.S., and not to mention a few things I don't tell my kids about.

It wasn't all fun and games though—I have seen highs and lows like everyone else, I have experienced poverty and risen above it, I have experienced serious illness and lived through it, and I have also spent some time fairly depressed, even angry. For example, it took me a long time to find a job after I received my graduate degree, and when I did find a job it was not quite what I had in mind, but it turned out to be a blessing. I was looking for more and started volunteering, but still the feeling of restlessness did not go away, and I was only in my early 30s. Though I was, and am still, happily married, I felt lonely. Looking at my life one might say I had everything, but I was still looking for something more. I had many friends and loving family, yet still no one to answer my burning questions about life such as, "how to be free?" I knew what I wanted it to look like but was not sure how to go about achieving it, as theory and reality are never the same. It is just like reading great reviews about a movie versus seeing it for yourself, or reviewing a recipe versus cooking—it can be different than how we imagine it to be.

I wanted to know how to start my journey towards this elusive peace. Who could teach me—who could show me the way? I searched far and wide. I wanted to continue to live my life as is and still begin a parallel path to inner peace and live life 200%. There was a hole in my life which nothing seemed to fill until I met my Guru…*sat[1]* Guru, a divine guide…who took away all my questions and showed me the path that led to inner peace. He taught me the tools for peace and happiness, and guided me to share this insight with you.

With this book I am sharing what I have learned after twenty-some years of seeking, researching, learning and, finally, experiencing inner calm/peace/bliss/ joy.

1 *Sat* Guru – one who is enlightened and can help others achieve the same

CHAPTER THREE

Ebb and Flow

"Time is like a flowing river, no water passes beneath your feet twice, much like the river, moments never pass you by again, so cherish every moment that life gives you."

~ Unknown

It is easier to have an attitude of gratitude when the events are happening the way we envision or plan them. We still feel good as long as the goal is in sight and attainable even if the roadmap has changed.

Challenge comes when our goal is not in sight and we have no idea what to do. We feel lost and life feels chaotic, we are way off the road we had planned to be on. Any kind of loss can do it to you whether it be a material or personal loss, and sometimes both happen at the same time. What can one say to someone who lost their job or is grieving for a loved one? What should one say or do?

My husband was part of the layoffs right after 9-11 when our children were young—one in high school and one in college. We had just bought a house and were a single income family. He was given a severance package, a handshake, and "good luck." He had worked for sixteen years at this corporation and had planned to retire from there. I could argue that he didn't deserve it and that he got caught in the crossfire, or that someone had it in for him and took advantage of the situation, and on and on. The bottom line is that someone in the organization decided that they didn't want or need him anymore. Whatever the reason, one fine day he called me from work in the morning, gave me the news, and told me today would be his last day at work.

I told him, "that's wonderful"—yes, that's exactly what I said—"come home and be with us. We are waiting for you and something will work out." My words were like a rope to a man sinking in quicksand. You are probably wondering, why wasn't I worried? Of course I was worried, but I also had faith that if we could start our lives in the U.S. with a few hundred dollars and without any family support, we would also get through this. There is something we are good at, and that is hard work, and hard work always pays off sometime or another.

That day my husband informed me that he would be home early, so I went to the grocery store and bought ingredients for his favorite meal and a bottle of champagne. By the time he got home, I had the table set up and champagne on ice. As he entered through the door into the house from the garage I was waiting for him with my best smile, love and assurance in my eyes and demeanor. I hugged him and held him and poured all the assurance into him making sure he felt loved and wanted.

Maybe he was expecting a weeping, worried, nagging wife, but I will never forget the look on his face as he entered and saw the bottle of champagne. His eyes were moist and he was speechless, the expression on his face too complex for words to do justice.

Before he could ask, I simply told him, "We are celebrating the beginning of the next chapter in our lives. When one door closes, another opens, you just have to be willing to walk through it with acceptance." He asked, "What do you mean?" I replied, "Accept the present however it is, and a way forward will come to you. It is the law of the universe. Without acceptance the way forward is extremely difficult because without acceptance one keeps going in circles and that's not the way forward." We talked into the wee hours that night and made new plans for our uncertain future.

My question to you is, "Is your future ever certain"?
          YES   NO

I am almost certain the sun will rise tomorrow morning, even though it may not be a sunny day. But I am not at all certain that I will live to see it—morbid, but true. We take our life for granted and at times work tirelessly towards a future which we may never live to see. Can you tell me for sure you will be alive to see whatever you are working towards? Let's make it simple; can you tell yourself for sure that you will live to see tomorrow or even the next moment? Nobody can. We hope to, but we can't be sure. 106.60 people die every minute, and 153,424.70 per day, according to the World Death Clock. All we have is this moment and it should be respected and fully appreciated. Our number could be up any minute.

Hence we decided to make our time count and associate ourselves with positive forces. We lost most friends who still worked at the same organization. It was as if we were contagious and they thought they may also lose their jobs by association. It's a perfectly normal response and we didn't begrudge them as everyone needs to pay bills. Many of our social friends felt sorry for us and did not know how to act around us or what to say. In the end we really had to prune our friendship tree. In times of crisis we needed only positive energy around us to encourage us and help us. We are fortunate to have parents who supported us from afar and some friends who stood with us and shared their network and tips from their experiences.

Over the years we had moved many times, sometimes nationally and at other times internationally, which was always challenging. But this was our first crisis of this magnitude together. We learned a lot from the process and were challenged in every way to hold onto the positive thoughts and keep the doubts at bay. It was not easy. We knew theoretically, and then first-hand, that life doesn't go as we plan or envision. We had read in so many places that life is ebb and flow. As part of the homework for one of my classes during my master's education, our professor asked us to draw a chart of our own life. This is what I drew for that homework assignment:

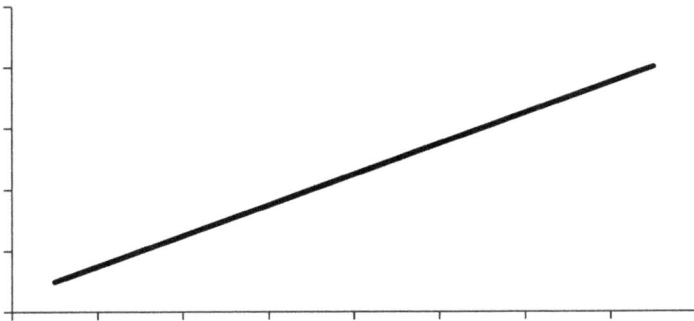

The professor called me in to her office and asked me to explain. I said, "My whole life has been evolving since my birth."

Professor: "Explain."

Me: "I was born, and then I got my education (high school and undergraduate), got married, and am now doing my graduate work."

Professor: "So you had no turbulence in life? Everything worked out perfectly?"

Me: "Of course not, I have seen more hardship than I should have at my age."

Professor: "How so?"

Me: "I was born in an upper middle class family and took the comforts of life for granted until we came to the U.S., where I have seen and lived below the poverty level."

Professor: "So how can you draw a straight line going up for your life?"

Me: "I thought you wouldn't be interested."

Professor: "That's the whole point—that line should reflect reality. To demonstrate that in life nothing ever goes only up as what goes up must come down, just like the market goes up and comes down; our heartbeat goes up and down. Everything is cyclical."

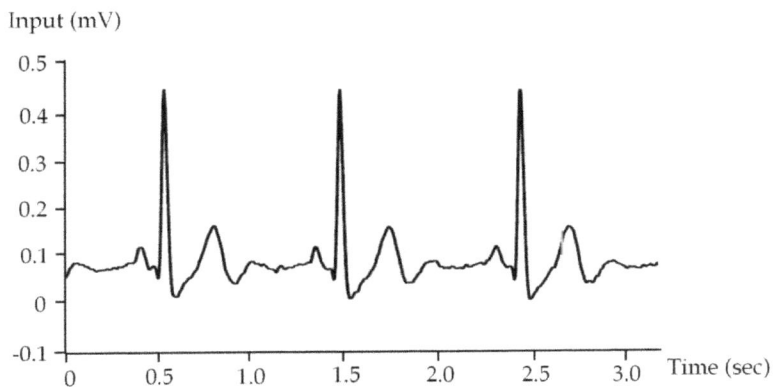

Heartbeat rhythm

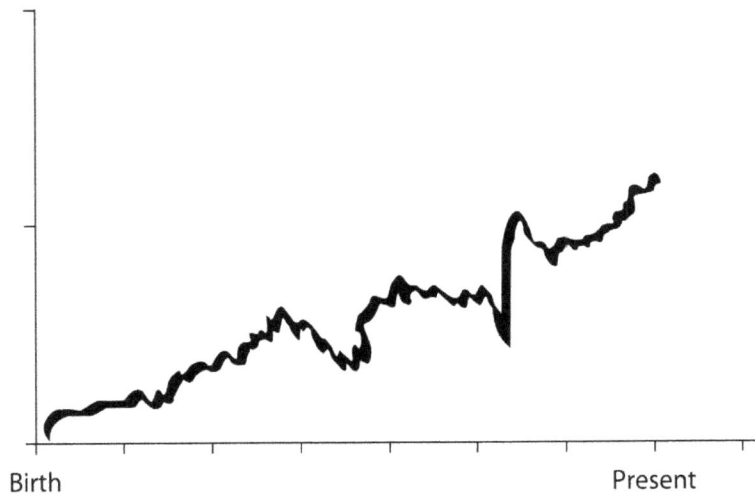

My second attempt at that homework

I was thankful to that professor for reminding me that it is normal for life to have ups and downs—in fact it's expected and it is evident all around us. Even plants need to go through a hibernation period to blossom again. Then why do the downs always surprise us? Our behavior at the time of crisis determines what our new height will be. Just like when an infant wants to walk—he usually masters crawling first, then while learning to walk he often falls and gradually gets better as his arms and legs get stronger and can hold his body weight. At this stage parents are there to encourage the infant to continue. If he gave up because he was afraid of falling or hurting himself he would not get to the next step of attempting to walk. At first he normally holds onto the table and other furniture in the room and gets comfortable with being vertical and moving. He leaves the security of furniture only out of necessity:

- To get to the goal
- To get to the encouraging parents who have been waiting for that first step with the proudest smiles
- To be free
- To be able to go around like older siblings and adults in the house

It is much slower to walk than it was to crawl at first but even to the infant, as slow as walking is, it's a new skill and a vertical view of the world, and worth the risk.

Watch the waves of any flowing water body. They go up and down and of course there are patches of calm water as well as rapids, but neither lasts forever. Even the air doesn't stay at the same speed. We have windy days, very windy days, calm days, still days, and we also have storms…

Everything is changeable and we must adapt with it. The

better we adapt, the more successful we become. Humans are the most evolved species because we continue to keep evolving with the circumstances. After my husband lost his job we also evolved with our circumstances because we had no choice. He worked at least eight hours a day, just like going to work, to look for a job. He kept polishing his resume, put his ego aside, and welcomed critique and suggestions from any and all. He followed every lead and learned to go beyond his comfort level. Our horizons were broadened because we were flexible in terms of our needs to be in a similar job. We let go of our expectations and landed a job and moved to another state.

Perhaps you can try to chart your life and observe the pattern.

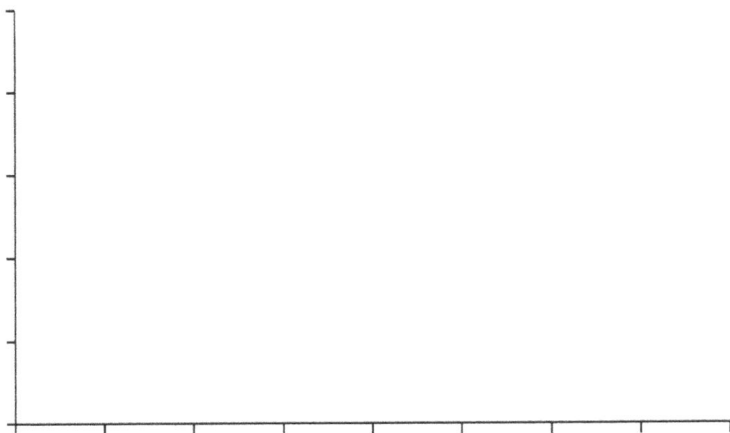

The biggest lesson we learned from this, one of the very difficult situations in life, was to not get tangled in the six-pronged mind—five W's: *who, what, when, where, why,* and an H: *how.*

Who has got it in for me?

What am I going to do now? Life's not fair.

When will I find a job? I have bills and house and car mortgages, how long can we eat from our savings?

Where will we end up?

Why me? I saved them millions, did great work, and was loyal.

How could they do this to me? I gave the best sixteen years of my life to the organization.

We had to be mindful of our expenses and aggressive in our job search, and at the same time keep our heads above *who, what, when, where, why and how.* It was not easy but regular breathing exercises helped to keep our bodies flowing with *prana*[2] and oxygen which helped us to be in the moment. It didn't let us get caught in the past, and allowed us to plan a path forward in pencil. A very wise man reminded us that the moon also goes through the waning and waxing period, and there is even no moon for one night and then the new moon continues to grow into that splendid full moon—that too is for one night only and in fourteen days we have no moon again. Everything that goes up must come down at some point. It is the Law of Nature/Universe/Gravity. This was and is a very powerful reminder to us and continues to help us stay positive through the trials of life.

---

2 *Prana* will be described in further detail in the "Power of Breath" chapter

This experience strengthened our ability to dive within for strength and not seek it outside. We are better for it and have braved many distresses in stride since then because that's what life is—developing the inner strength to handle and manage life's crises. You have what it takes to be what you want to be. All you have to do is look within. The first step is paying attention to your breathing so that you can live in the present moment.

I became more regular in practicing yoga and *pranayama*[3] for the mental benefits and for the power and strength breathing offers me to go within and deal with whatever life throws at me. I will be talking more about breathing throughout this book and in more detail in the "Power of Breath" chapter.

The mind likes to be occupied, so give it an occupation of your choice rather than that of chaos, one that will help you be at peace. To begin, allow your mind to follow your breath without changing your breathing pattern for 3-5 minutes.

- Close your eyes
- Follow your breath
- Observe the inhalation and follow the air going in from your nose or mouth
- Notice if your chest expands or not
- Notice how the breath feels going in
- Explore the path of the inhalation
- Notice the calmness that is descending upon you
- Deepen your inhale slowly and steadily
- Hold your breath a moment

---

3 *Pranayama* will be described in further detail in the "Power of Breath" chapter

- Exhale slowly and completely at the same rate as inhalation
- Notice if it feels any different coming out than going in
- Repeat a few deep breaths and enjoy the calmness

Deep breathing and focusing on the moment highlighted for us that circumstances are just circumstances—that's it. No more, no less. It is what we make of them that counts. Nothing is constant. Every night has a morning no matter how dark and every day has a night no matter how sunny. If things don't seem to be going the right way, they will eventually improve, and if they are going very well, that may not last forever either. There is no growth without ups and downs.

Look around you in nature. Most trees have a growth spurt in spring and they bloom full all summer, and then come autumn the leaves change color and in winter they fall. The tree goes dormant and all we have are branches with their own stark beauty. The cycle continues even in death. Next time you walk in the woods, notice how the fallen, dead trees are at different stages of becoming part of the forest floor. They are becoming part of the bigger cycle as they provide nutrients to the nascent plants.

"We have no control over our circumstances
—only how we deal with them

We have no control over the wind
—only our sail, which we can adjust

We have no control over the weather outside
—only our thermostat

We have no control over others' words
—only our reaction to them

Your present circumstances determine your starting
point—your actions will determine where you go."

~ Unknown

CHAPTER FOUR

Elephant Walks, Dogs Bark

"Life is simple, but we insist on making it complicated."

~ Confucius

I am in the habit of observing the nature around me, including animals. I find walking barefoot on the grass to be a great way to communicate with Mother Earth, as well as to recharge myself and get rid of toxins. This is a simple, refreshing way to purge yourself, rather than using different mud or spa wraps, because you can stretch your limbs and be grateful for the ability to do so at the same time. Yes, I am one of those silly people you might see hugging a tree in a park and talking to it. When you start paying attention to the nature around you, you will find that it communicates with you and imparts wisdom all the time.

Have you ever noticed little sparrows hovering at the heels of hawks in the air? It is amazing how these little birds try to pursue hawks, try to fly just as high, even pecking at the hawks' tails or wings until the hawks are out of reach. The most interesting fact of this occurrence is that even though the hawks have the ability to squash or injure these delicate, stubborn little sparrows—they don't. They don't even acknowledge them. Rather they keep soaring higher and higher, and eventually the sparrows fall back and have no choice but to go about their own business.

Elephants behave in a somewhat similar fashion to hawks. They rarely do anything to call attention to themselves. They are so majestic that we pay attention to them of our own accord because we cannot help it. During my travels to India I had an extended stay at an Ashram on the banks of the Ganges and had the privilege of observing forest wildlife in its natural habitat—something one does not witness every day in the city.

At the Ashram, as at home, I typically meditate at dawn or dusk. Since I am so fascinated with the animal kingdom, my Guru asked me to meditate in natural surroundings with my eyes open. This not only introduced me to a new way of meditation, but also taught me a lot—Mother Nature is our best teacher. There is something to be learned, from a blade of grass to a giant sequoia tree, from an ant to an elephant. All we have to do is observe and silence our minds so that we can listen and learn.

Years ago, Baba (my Guru) would repeatedly tell me, "Be like a blade of grass," and then not explain further. His intent was to help calm me. However it often had the opposite effect as I did not understand what he was trying to convey and would become frustrated. He did not explain the meaning of his message outright, because when we figure something out on our own, it is a more meaningful lesson. The meaning is understood more deeply because we have contemplated and digested the query and its implications thoroughly.

After contemplating Baba's request to "be like a blade of grass," I went back to him and told him I understood what it means. He happily asked me to explain:

I said, "Grass always grows back every season."

Baba: "Every kind of grass?"

Me: "I have lived in the Midwest for most of my life, so from my personal experience I know that all grass varieties do not survive excessive heat, cold, or drought. In fact, only a few survive all kinds of extreme weather and come back season after season—whether it be after a polar vortex or a hot and dry summer."

Baba: "What else do you know about grass?"

Me: "Grass grows back after mowing no matter how close to the ground you mow it."

Baba: "Why?"

I had to think about this question, as this phenomena was something I had observed decade after decade without giving it any particular thought, so I said, "Because of the wide, deep and interconnected root system."

Baba: "Okay... in a storm what kind of tree or plant would you want to be?"

I thought this one was easy as I had taught it in my management classes, and it is mentioned in many places, and told him, "We want to be like a palm tree because it is flexible and can sway with the winds, whereas a mighty oak tree is rigid and at a greater risk of breaking a branch or being uprooted."

Baba: "Very good—what happens if an elephant comes?"

I was stumped now as I had not thought that far. As I thought about it, I realized that an elephant could easily uproot a palm tree and would have a harder time doing so with bigger, sturdier trees. Suddenly, I did not have an answer.

Baba: "What about a blade of grass? Would it survive the elephant and the storm?"

After much contemplation I said, "Yes, because even an

elephant or storm cannot uproot grass. Even if the soil is uprooted with grass, the grass would survive in its new place. Grass could survive an elephant's weight if it walked on it and even if it were to sit on the grass for a period of time—the grass would be upright again, and seemingly unaffected, within a few minutes after the elephant departed."

Baba: "Is grass of any use to us?"

This one I could answer.

Me: "Wild grass, like prairie land, is an important part of our eco system and home to many insects, birds, and even small animals. We all enjoy grass in our backyards with our families, grass on the golf course is soothing to the eyes, and grass in the parks is important especially for children to play, and so many animals eat grass.…"

He was satisfied with my answer, but I had not thought of grass like that before—a plant which I had not thought significant is not only so unassuming and hardy, but also gives without expecting anything in return and takes everything in stride. Each blade of grass is so sure in itself—AMAZING!

Baba's ultimate message was to observe and learn. To be like a mighty blade of grass is not an easy feat.

Since then, I try to embody and practice being like a blade of grass:

- It reminds me that I can withstand the storms of my life gracefully
- It reminds me to tap into my inner strength during the trying times of life—that my roots are deep and wide
- It gives me immense strength to acknowledge that even if I am uprooted I will thrive in my new

environment
- No matter what life throws at me, I can handle it
- Most importantly, similar to grass, I can provide joy and comfort to others by just being myself

So much to learn from a blade of grass—makes you wonder how much there is to learn from Mother Nature, and find peace at the same time.

My favorite times of the day have always been, and remain, dawn and dusk. Nature is awakening at dawn and one can feel the high vibrations and the urgency in the atmosphere. Even the color display in the sky is spectacular—interestingly, every sunrise has the same colors but it is different from day to day and region to region, simply amazing. Dusk is an equally high vibration time of day when the sun is setting and casting a beautiful array of colors in the sky, and welcoming the night so that nature and its inhabitants alike can rest from the activities of the day and recharge during sleep. Birds fly to their nests and create nighttime music; critters settle down; and the night animals, birds, and mosquitoes create a different kind of softer melody to lull our senses. The stars and moon in the sky add wonder and beauty to the night.

This is what was intended for us before electricity. I remember my childhood visits, at the age of eleven or twelve, to my old fashioned grandparents during the summer holidays. Our day started with a walk at five o'clock A.M. at sunrise, followed by yoga, and ended with dinner at dusk followed by sleeping on cots under the moon and stars, listening to my grandmother's stories. We slept outside because there was no air conditioner. But it was the best time of the day for me— looking at the stars and wondering about them, listening to my grandmother telling stories. I remember it as a very peaceful time.

Back to my travels in India at the Ashram, during my open eye meditations with nature at sunrise or sunset, I would often notice a herd of elephants coming to bathe, drink and play at the Ganges shore. It was very enlightening and fascinating to observe them, because they all played nicely as a unit but were independent at the same time. They did not bother or hurt the other species in the water around them, which were much smaller in size. Interestingly, every evening, a pack of wild dogs would also show up and start barking at them. The dogs would bark from a distance at first, and then they would move closer to about five feet away, bark again, then run back and bark, and then go close and bark again. They would continue this ritual for quite some time. I don't know if the dogs were trying to scare the elephants or just get attention. They never went into the water, probably because the current was so swift. They would just bark for a while and then eventually go away.

Meanwhile, the elephants went about their ritual of playing and spraying water on each other and themselves until it got too hot or too dark. It was impressive that even baby elephants did not pay attention to the wild dogs or any other lifeforms around them. They were focused. After they were done, the elephants went back up the path into the mountains.

At times when we are trying to focus on something important, trying to move away from a bad situation or developing a new, positive way of life, old thoughts can creep up on us from all sides. At that time it helps me to think of myself as an elephant that has the ability to ignore the annoying wild dogs (annoying thoughts), or as a hawk who soars without paying attention to the pesky sparrows (unwanted thoughts). Or even as a blade of grass, that quickly rises again after being trampled.

There will always be people who support us and there will always be some who will try and bring us down— this is a fact of life that we must accept

From time to time, I feel a pull from too many annoying directions that have the ability to distract me. Time is a luxury we don't have, so I picture myself as an elephant and all the distractions, human or mental, as wild dogs trying to interfere with my playtime. Picturing myself as an elephant immediately puts me in charge of my mind and helps me stay focused on the task at hand.

One of my students (we will call him Tom) is an executive in a mid-sized corporation. His demeanor is gently strong— gentle, but firm; kind, but not a pushover. He believes that one doesn't have to raise one's voice to show authority. He also believes that a resolution can be achieved calmly, without having a screaming match. He believes in creative freedom and mutual respect. Another executive (Sam) whom Tom has to interact with every day has a very different personality. He is aggressive, loud, and controlling. Tom found it trying to work with Sam because of his loud mouth and his habit of swearing all the time. Sam believes that raising one's voice, calling people out in front of everyone, and being very loud and demanding is manly behavior—anything else is being weak or passive. This is a difficult situation for both of them—they are both nice people but with very different communication styles.

In one of our many conversations, I shared my story of the elephants with Tom. As soon as he heard it, he started laughing, and pretty soon we were both laughing. Now whenever he is in a difficult situation with Sam he pictures himself as an elephant, which allows him to feel more solid and large in stature, and prevents him from reacting to Sam while at the same time enabling him to listen and get work done. This way Sam is satisfied that he has been heard and can also conduct his business in his style, and both are happy. Nobody reacts and work gets done.

This process is very simple—try this visual exercise:

- Close your eyes
- Take three deep breaths
- Pay attention to your breath as you inhale
- Watch as you exhale
- Take three more deep breaths
- Continue to "watch" your breath
- Visualize yourself as an elephant
- Feel that you are as big and solid as the elephant
- Feel the quiet assurance and wisdom of the elephant within you
- Observe yourself ignoring the barking dogs/ distracting thoughts begging for your attention, choosing to engage only when needed
- Feel the deep smile that comes from within… stay with it…
- Be comfortable with your inner strength and the power that comes from not reacting
- Stay as an elephant for as long as needed and become one as often as you like—and take charge of your mind

You have now taken control of, and have power over, your mind and thoughts

Ask yourself a question:

Can you ignore the barking dogs/irritating thoughts?
YES   NO

This exercise can be repeated with the hawk and sparrows visualization, as well:

- Close your eyes
- Take three deep breaths
- Pay attention to your breath as you inhale
- Watch as you exhale
- Take three more deep breaths
- Continue to "watch" your breath
- Visualize yourself as a hawk taking flight from the ground
- Enjoy the freedom of flight and feel the air currents around you
- Observe the pesky sparrows nipping at your heels
- Feel the current of wind around you and soar with it, go higher
- Ignore the sparrows/distracting thoughts, continue with your flight and take on the air current to go higher, choosing to engage only when needed
- Observe everyone from this vantage point
- Feel the deep smile that comes from within... stay with it...
- Be comfortable with your inner strength and the

power that comes from not reacting
- Stay as a hawk for as long as needed and become one as often as you like—and take charge of your mind

Most people feel calm after this visualization, and become aware of their inner strength to deal with the difficult situations.

Baba, my Guru, would often tell the story of the "Turtle & Scorpion." It is one you may have heard as a child:

Once, a scorpion needed to cross the river but could not because of his limitation of being unable to swim. He asked many swimming animals to help him, but they all refused because they were afraid he would sting them despite his promises not to. Finally, the scorpion approached a kind hearted and trusting turtle that was going to cross the river to visit his family. The turtle was naturally hesitant due to the scorpion's poisonous sting, and refused. But the scorpion was persistent as he too wanted to visit his family. So he appealed to the turtle's sense of family. The turtle felt sorry for him and agreed to take him to the other side of the river if the scorpion promised not to sting him.

Although the turtle agreed, he was quite afraid. But an agreement was an agreement, and so they started their journey. Midway, the turtle felt the scorpion getting ready to sting and quickly reminded him of his promise, and also that if he stung him they would both drown. At that reminder the scorpion stopped. The pair continued at a slow, steady pace towards the other side of the river. When they were almost to the shore, the scorpion stung the turtle and hopped off. The turtle was shocked at the scorpion's actions—not keeping his word, and using and killing him in the process. The turtle asked the scorpion, "WHY?" The scorpion replied, "It is in my nature. I cannot help it."

We all give what we have. It is very difficult to go against our developed nature. All kinds of people make up the composition of this world. An angry person has only anger to give, a sarcastic person can only be sarcastic, a happy person spreads joy, and a kind person will continue to be kind even against his better judgment—because that is his developed nature.

Our innate nature is actually to be happy and loving; however, our conditions can change how we act. It is up to us to be aware of how we have become, and work towards becoming a peaceful and loving person again. However, it is important to remember that we cannot change the nature of others, and must learn to accept them for who they are.

We control only our own behavior

The next time you are trying something new, finishing up something, or trying to forgive or forget and pesky thoughts keep intruding or wild things try to distract you, experiment with this visualization: soar away like a hawk or walk majestically like an elephant. You would be pleasantly surprised how well this works.

CHAPTER FIVE

Power of Breath

"When you own your breath, nobody can steal your peace."

~ Unknown

Breathing is essential to our survival, yet we pay the least amount of attention to it. Most of us are on autopilot when it comes to breathing. We typically get enough air to survive, but not to revitalize us. Can you remember the refreshing feeling you experience when you go out in fresh air and take in a deep lungful breath, and how alive you suddenly feel? Why rely on memory when you can experience it right now.

On a scale of 1 to 5 how do you feel right now? _____

Now step outside and take a deep breath, inhaling as much as you can through your nose and then exhale fully. Take a few deep breaths. Feel free to close your eyes. Come back inside whenever you are ready.

On a scale of 1-5 how much better do you feel in comparison to before you took the deep breaths outside? _____

"He lives most life whoever breathes most air."

~ Elizabeth Barrett Browning

There is a reason that the deep lungful of air makes such a big difference in how you feel. You just manipulated the way you normally breathe. In that manipulation of breathing you inhaled more than oxygen, and you got a lungful of *Prana* as well—which is part of the reason you are feeling so alive now. Optimum oxygen levels help the physiology of our body, and optimum *Prana* levels help our psyche. There are numerous studies on the direct relationship between our overall wellness and the oxygen levels in the body. There is one sure way to raise the oxygen levels in our body quickly and that is through abdominal breathing, which I will explain in more detail in this chapter. Abdominal breathing also raises *Prana* in our body, thereby improving our overall function.

What is Prana?

I asked this question myself when I first heard of it. The literal translation of *Prana* is "life force." I had heard of *Prana* growing up, but I never inquired about it, because I associated it with death.... Lack of *Prana* means no life. I again heard of the word *Prana* when I started learning a form of yoga, *Pranayama* or *Raj Yoga*, from my yoga teacher several years ago. He would narrate stories of Yogis living hundreds of very healthy years as a result of practicing *Pranayama*. Of course, I did not believe this in the beginning, because my logical and analytical mind assumed that was simply not possible.

However, after much time as one of the students of my yoga teacher and learning the science of *Prana* and the role it plays in our body, it became a believable possibility. Once it became a possibility, all of us students wanted to learn and understand *Pran, Prana,* and *Pranayama.*

We knew the basics: *Prana* is a Sanskrit word. Sanskrit is the oldest language in the world. The literal translation of

Prana is:

> *Prana*: pra + ana
>
> *pra*: prior, or to have prior existence
>
> *ana*: an atom or a singular element which exists in
> everything

> In Chinese, it is known as *chi*
>
> In Japanese, it is known as *ki*
>
> In Polynesian, it is known as *mana*

But this information did not really answer the question of what this mysterious *Prana* is and why it is so important. We would ask our yoga teacher, "What is *Prana*?"

He would reply, "That is a difficult question to answer. After all we cannot see *Prana*, or touch, smell, taste, or hear it. It is in the air but it is neither air nor one of the chemical constituents of air—i.e. nitrogen, oxygen, argon, carbon dioxide, water vapor, neon, helium, methane, etc. But it is there and we breathe it in along with the oxygen, and yet, it is not oxygen."

Our next question was, "If we assume *Prana* is in the atmosphere, why do we need it?" To answer that question he shared some history of *Prana*. It is mentioned in scriptures from 300 – 5000 BC, like the *Upanishads* and *Vedanta Sutras*. He then told us the enlightening story of the five senses, including Breath (and *Prana*), from the *Chandogya Upanishad*, which left no room for further questions.

To summarize the story: Once five of the senses of human nature—Mind, Breath (source of *Prana*), Speech, Ears (hearing ability) and Eyes (sight)—were arguing as to which one was the most essential sense. This reflects the usual state of humans—our senses are not integrated and compete within us for attention.

To settle this dispute once and for all they decided that each would leave the body for a specific period of time and then see which one was missed the most.

First, eyesight left for some time and the body continued on with life, though blind. Then, ears left for a year and the body continued on, though deaf. Next, speech left and the body still lived, though mute. Then the mind left and the body continued, though dumb. Finally, when the breathing stopped and *Prana* started to leave, all the other senses started to die and they then understood that without *Prana,* or life-force energy, the body cannot function. Clearly, *Prana* won the dispute of the senses. But to inhale optimum *Prana,* we must breathe properly.

When a person dies, we hesitate to touch them no matter how close we were to them, no matter how much we loved them or how devoted we were to them, even though it is the same body that we may have hugged a few moments before. All the body parts are still there, including the forever-ruling mind, but there is no heartbeat so that individual is declared dead. What changes? The person has the same face, same limbs, same organs, etc., just no heartbeat. I have heard people at a viewing say, "He seemed so lifelike, I expected him to wake up and talk to me," but lifelike and alive are life and death apart.

What makes our heart beat? What is it that gives the ability to our brain to function, our limbs to move, our eyes to see, our ears to hear, our vascular system to function…what is it that makes us alive? These questions used to gnaw at me in my childhood and I would ask anyone who would listen. Everyone had an answer but nothing quite sat right with me.

One day I was told, "It is life that makes you alive." I could live with that answer as it made perfect sense to me then, and still does. It is LIFE that makes me ALIVE. This concept helped me grasp that LIFE is neither body nor brain nor mind. It is not necessary for LIFE to be visible per say, but it can be felt and experienced. I understood that it is that special something that makes humans, animals, plants and every species alive. That something is called *PRANA* in Sanskrit which translates as life force energy. It is that *Prana* that makes our heart beat and makes us alive. The amazing reality is that *Prana* is the same in everyone, in every species and in every race.

Basics of breathing

It is a scientific fact that the cells in our body require oxygen to function. Therefore our physical health is directly related to how well we breathe. It is our circulatory system that takes fresh red blood from the heart out to every corner of our body and brings blue blood full of toxins back for purification. It is the lungs that are responsible for using oxygen to purify the blood, and remove all the waste that the cells need to expel. In any given day, approximately 35,000 pints of blood pass through the lungs with the hopes of coming into contact with oxygen to pass life back to every cell in the body.

Imagine what would happen if there was not enough oxygen to go around. Without oxygen our bodies could not metabolize food and perform other important functions, such as keeping our nervous system healthy. Without enough oxygen, the blood that is circulated back to the body already contains toxins that could be spread again or limit the capacity of the circulatory system to remove more toxins from the body. Either way, a fully healthy body isn't possible in this scenario. I know it can be hard to picture blood pumping through the body, so imagine the air filtration system in your house or at work. Anytime you turn the heat or air conditioning on, air passes through the filter as it gets heated or cooled in the furnace/HVAC system. If this is a high quality filter (a really deep breath, rich with oxygen) it removes allergens, dust, mites, etc. from the air, but if it's a low quality filter (a shallow breath of air) it only catches a small portion of the harmful elements in the air and they settle down in the corners of the house. If these allergens collect in the house, they cause other problems like allergies, or in extreme cases, respiratory issues. If you had a simple way to avoid such problems, wouldn't you pursue it?

There are many publications that are dedicated only to breathing which can help you gain a deeper understanding, but there are a few things I would like to highlight regarding the science of breathing, in a very simplistic way.

The importance of breathing through your nose

You have probably heard or read that it is important to breathe through your nose, not your mouth, for two main reasons. First, the nose is equipped to filter dust and pollutants and regulate the temperature of the air we inhale to optimize the lungs' ability to draw oxygen and expel carbon dioxide. Second, the nose acts as a forcing mechanism to control the air flow volume to maintain the proper balance of oxygen and carbon dioxide. As you know, the nose has a smaller diameter than the mouth, forcing the lungs to inhale and exhale at a slower rate. This allows the lungs to take the time to extract more oxygen and release more carbon dioxide with each breath.

Take the time to pay attention to your breathing, to see if you breathe more through your nose or mouth. Practice breathing through your nose, and notice changes in how you generally feel. I have had a few students tell me that this is simply not possible because they have allergies or sinus problems, or generally, their nose is usually blocked preventing them from breathing through their nose. I tell all of them the same thing, "start small." Start with forcing breath through your nose a few minutes a day and you will slowly notice that it becomes easier; in fact, the congestion decreases over time. The natural state of our breathing is through the nose, and in conjunction with allergy medicine, focused breathing would help improve air flow through the nose and reduce congestion.

Proper breathing can enhance the quality of life

Deep breathing

Deep breathing is enabled by the contraction of the diaphragm (a horizontal muscle located between the chest cavity and stomach cavity), to allow room for the lungs to expand.

One type of deep breathing known as diaphragmatic breathing makes full use of this muscle to maximize lung expansion. When breathing in, the diaphragm contracts, which means the stomach pushes up as the lungs fill with air. On exhalation, the diaphragm returns to normal position, and the stomach returns to its normal state, putting pressure on the lungs to force air out. If the chest or stomach is contracting on inhaling, this is a sign that the lungs aren't getting the chance to fully expand, and you should try to consciously adapt your breathing to support maximum lung expansion.

Another type of deep breathing is known as rolling or complete deep breathing. This method of breathing is not something that is typically done all day long, like diaphragmatic breathing, rather at times when your goal is to sit and focus on your breathing—whether as a part of meditation, yoga or simply stress relief. This method of breathing can be thought of as adding on to the diaphragmatic breathing. You begin the same way by inhaling and pushing out/expanding your stomach, but once your stomach feels stretched, continue to inhale and feel your chest expanding too. Feel your chest expand and your shoulders move back as you push your lungs to expand and elongate but also inflate outwards. When you exhale, you'll feel both your chest and stomach return to normal position—make sure to use the diaphragm again to create pressure on the lungs to fully exhale the carbon dioxide heavy air.

In this day and age we are caught up in the web of 'faster and still faster' economic development and technology progression, where life is becoming more and more impersonal and stressful. Mindful breathing offers us a much needed respite. It increases our EQ (Emotional Quotient) by helping us be in the present and enjoy better physical and mental health.

It also increases our IQ (Intelligence Quotient) and EQ (Emotional Quotient) by helping us be calm and focused, creative and energetic, as well as by improving memory. It increases our overall wellbeing by helping us find balance.

As naturally as breathing comes to us, proper breathing may seem unnatural at first because we are used to breathing in a certain way. It will eventually become part of you as it is the way we were born breathing. Observe the breathing of a sleeping infant. He epitomizes diaphragmatic breathing. When inhaling his abdomen extends, his chest expands and his collar bone rises, and when exhaling his tummy contracts all the way. We were all born with this ability, but somewhere along the way we stopped being aware of our breath and breathing pattern. An infant is very aware of his breath and himself.

I use many breathing/*pranayama* exercises to teach mindful breathing to my students. Mindful breathing is best taught in person, and I am providing a breathing and *pranayama* exercise in this chapter to give you an initial taste. It is best to read the exercises a few times and fully understand the sequence before completing them to ensure maximum benefit. If nothing else, follow one simple rule when breathing:

While inhaling your abdomen should extend and ribcage should expand, while exhaling your abdomen should contract. Do not try to extend your abdomen artificially.

If you are unsure, please contact your health provider before attempting to change your breathing pattern.

If you feel discomfort when breathing at any time, stop and contact your health provider if the discomfort persists.

Complete deep breathing exercise:

After reading the below guidelines, find a comfortable place to sit or lie down. Make sure you are wearing comfortable clothing. Most people feel energetic and calm after this exercise.

- If sitting, sit with your spine straight, feet touching the floor gently
- Place your hands on your knees and relax your shoulders
- If lying down, keep legs shoulder width apart, arms by your side, palms down and feel the surface under your body
- Close your eyes and observe yourself
- Feel the chair under your hips
- Feel the floor under your feet
- Feel the weight of your hands on your knees
- Inhale slowly and steadily through your nostrils into your lungs and feel your diaphragm contracting
- As your inhalation continues feel your lower ribs, breastbone and chest pushing out
- As you inhale feel your upper chest rising including the upper six or seven pairs of ribs lifting
- In the final movement your abdomen may be slightly drawn in, giving lungs support
- Hold the breath for a few seconds
- Exhale quite slowly holding the chest in a firm position
- Draw in your abdomen a little, lifting it upwards slowly as the air leaves the lungs

Repeat 3-5 times. You might feel a little dizzy the first few times as your brain is not used to so much oxygen and is feeling the natural high. Observe how you feel…. Do not perform this complete deep breathing exercise outside your home or right before driving.

It is important to note that the inhalation should be continuous; the entire chest cavity from the lower diaphragm to the highest point of the chest should be expanded in a fluid movement. Similarly, the exhalation should also be a slow yet continuous process. Deep abdominal breathing improves our physical and mental wellbeing. When our mind is unsteady and thinking negative thoughts, we can easily turn the tide by practicing:

- Observing ourselves
- Deep abdominal breathing
- Accepting and loving ourselves

When you control your
Breath, you control everything

We are constantly inhaling air charged with Prana and extracting *Prana*, the life force energy. The natural atmosphere has a higher amount of *Prana* compared to our insulated homes. When we move away from the city to a park, forest, mountain peak or body of water, we instinctively breathe more deeply because deep down we have that understanding of inhaling *Prana*.

Our subconscious knows to absorb the abundance of *Prana* in nature and store it in the nerve center for later use. In basic breathing we absorb and extract the normal supply of *Prana*. With controlled and regulated breathing, also known as *Pranayama*, we are able to extract a greater supply of Prana and absorb more for later use.

I think of *Pranayama* as a workout for the central nervous system, a way for our nerves to be cleansed and charged. The oxygen in the air is appropriated by blood and used by the circulatory system so that oxygenated blood can be carried to all parts of the system. *Prana* in the air is appropriated by the nervous system, adding strength and vitality to our bodies. Every thought, every act, every effort of will, and every motion of muscle uses up a certain amount of what I call nerve force, which is a form of *Prana.*

We need a decent amount of *Prana* to merely exist, as every brain command for our daily existence uses nerve force. It makes sense to store as much *Prana* as possible to have an abundance of positive life force. Anyone who has mastered the science of storing *Prana*, either consciously or subconsciously, radiates vitality and strength, which is felt by all those whom come in contact with that person.

By now you must want to know how to increase your *Prana* storage. That can be done by practicing *Pranayama.*

Pranayama is a deliberate modification of the breathing process. One makes the respiratory organs move and expand intentionally, rhythmically and intensively. In this ancient method there is a long, sustained flow of inhalation, exhalation and retention of breath. Thus the flow of *Prana* is regulated along with thoughts, desires and actions, which give poise and tremendous will power to master oneself. ~ Iyenger

Pranayama exercise:
There are three basic ways of modifying the breathing process for *Pranayama*:
- By inhaling and exhaling slowly
- By inhaling and exhaling rapidly
- By holding the breath before and after exhalation

Things to keep in mind before attempting Pranayama:

- You may wish to consult a health professional before starting *Pranayama*
- Proper training: as mentioned earlier, this is just to give you an initial taste and not a substitute for proper training. You could enquire at your Yoga studio if they teach *Pranayama*
- Selection of place: it is best if performed in the same place every day and in fresh air, if possible
- Time of practice: early morning on an empty stomach and must wait half an hour after completion before eating or drinking
- Diet and food habits: light food intake is preferred
- Combination of *Pranayama* with other activities
- Regularity of practice: daily practice is most helpful
- A clear nasal passage: if stuffy do not practice *pranayama*
- Suitable posture: sit with spine straight on floor or on a chair

Exercise:
- Take three deep abdominal breaths
- Take one complete breath as outlined earlier
- Close your right nostril with your right thumb and inhale deeply and slowly from the left nostril
- Close left nostril with middle or ring finger and exhale slowly and completely from right nostril
- Inhale slowly and deeply with right nostril then close right nostril

- Exhale slowly and completely from left nostril
- Repeat 3-5 times
- You may feel a little light headed so stay seated for few minutes

Most people find practicing Pranayama helps them:

- To find the power of now
- To be calm and focused
- To be creative and energetic
- To enhance memory
- To improve physical and mental health
- To find balance in life
- To have a *positive outlook*

To find serenity – that no-stress calm state – we must calm the storm through deep deliberate breathing

CHAPTER SIX

Vibrations

"Just because you don't understand it, doesn't mean it isn't so."
~ Lemony Snicket

In this modern age we all take electricity for granted, as it is the foundation of our day to day living. Electricity is not a human invention. Even in remote areas of the world lacking power grids, electricity still exists—whether in storm clouds or even in the human nervous system. Even though advancements in practical applications of electricity were not made until the late nineteenth century, electric phenomena have always existed.

Thanks to numerous scientists we are able to harness that energy into an electric current, and take simple and complex pleasures of life for granted. For example, electricity allows us many comforts—from simply reading comfortably in bed after hours to keeping the house warm or cold. On a grander scale, as a result of electricity we can travel to all corners of the world, instantly communicate with anyone in any time zone, and so on.

Einstein introduced the famous equation $E=mc^2$, which correlates energy and mass to allow for the calculation of the energy equivalence of any amount of mass. This equation tells us in mathematical terms that mass (including you and me) is energy. We learn in school that nuclear energy is very powerful, that an atom, not even visible to the naked eye, provides powerful amounts of energy. Although similar technology has also allowed for the negative use of energy, such as the creation of atomic bombs, its essence is still energy. We also know that matter vibrates. According to the Merriam Webster dictionary, vibration is "a periodic motion of the particles of an elastic body or medium in alternately opposite directions." Therefore, when particles like atoms or water molecules are moving they are vibrating—and creating energy.

Everything is energy—you, me, your family, your pets, your friends, your home, your vehicle, your desk, your computer, a speck of dirt, plants, rocks, mountains, oceans, rivers, ponds—everything from a human to a needle to a spaceship to the elements—is made up of energy. That also means that everything is vibrating—you are vibrating, everything around you is vibrating, everyone around you is vibrating—we are all vibrating and vibrations keep changing. While we don't see vibrations in ourselves or others, we can feel them.

When you say "I have a lot of energy today" you are vibrating at a higher level. When you feel sluggish, sad, sick, or simply not very well, you are vibrating at a lower level. In fact, when you feel good every mechanism in your body is in sync. All your organs are working harmoniously resulting in feel-good high vibrations which equates a higher energy level.

Here is a quick experiment for you to try:

Part I
- Close your eyes and take three full deep breaths
- Say the following to yourself, out loud or in your head, with complete conviction:
    - o I feel great
    - o I feel wonderful
    - o I have everything I need
    - o I feel so blessed
- Repeat three times with more and more conviction each time
- Open your eyes

Examine how you feel and write it down:
- ☐ Wonderful
- ☐ Peaceful
- ☐ Great
- ☐ Better than before
- ☐ Same as before
- ☐ Worse than before
- ☐ Other _____

Part II

- Close your eyes and take a full deep breath
- Say the following to yourself, out loud or in your head, with complete conviction:
  - o I feel lousy/miserable
  - o I feel useless
  - o I need _____ (fill in the blank with something you want)
  - o I feel like life has cheated me
- Repeat three times with more and more conviction each time
- Open your eyes

Examine how you feel and write it down:
- ☐ Better than before
- ☐ Same as before
- ☐ A little worse
- ☐ A lot worse
- ☐ Depressed
- ☐ Like the air has been sucked out of me
- ☐ Other _____

Personally, I am starting to feel my vibration levels decrease by just writing these words....

Power of Thought - this demonstrates how powerful you are. Your thoughts are energy. You can make clean energy and be happy, joyful and at peace while spreading the same feeling around you, or you can make a bomb of negative energy and allow your thoughts to be destructive towards yourself and others around you.

The choice is yours

Since everything is energy, I am sure you have felt and reacted to it. Think about the people in your life that you like being around more than others; why is that? What kind of people do you dislike being around?

Use the following exercise to help you—list the names of at least five people you like and dislike being around, along with the reasons why:

People you like being around   Why?

1.

2.

3.

4.

5.

People you dislike being around   Why?

1.

2.

3.

4.

5.

Do you see any similarities in the reasons amongst the two groups?

I have been doing this same experiment with people for years and the results are reassuringly similar. The top five reasons people like being around someone were because that person:

- Made them feel good
- Smiled often
- Didn't complain
- Didn't criticize
- Had a positive attitude

The top five reasons people do not like being around someone were because that person:

- Complained all the time
- Criticized all the time
- Talked only about negative things
- Was sarcastic, manipulative, or shouted a lot
- Ignored others, thinking they are better than everyone around them

This makes perfect sense because your own vibration levels changed for a moment with the way you thought about the individuals in your life.

Thoughts can impact you in powerful ways. Below is another scientific explanation which will help further demonstrate the power of thought.

Think for a moment about water—what image comes to mind? Rain, a pond, a swimming pool, a lake, or perhaps an ocean? It is a peaceful feeling to think of a water body—even if people don't like being in the water, almost everyone likes being near a waterbody. How about your own body? We all know that in the human body, water is the most abundant chemical compound, accounting for 65-90% of each cell. Each water molecule consists of two hydrogen atoms bonded with one oxygen atom. The average human body can survive only 3-5 days without water. Not very long, is it?

Dr. Masaru Emoto, an internationally renowned researcher and entrepreneur, has done extensive research on the effect of emotion on the crystal formation of water. He has successfully demonstrated the effect of words on water through his experiments. For example, in one of his experiments, the photographs taken of water frozen after being placed in four different glass containers with words taped to the sides clearly demonstrated how words impacted crystal formation.

Positive words like "love and gratitude," "peace," "exhilaration," "I can do it," "happiness," etc. produced beautiful, equally formed crystals like lovely snowflakes. However, words like "dislike", "ugly," "it is hopeless," "isolate," "ignore," etc. produced irregular and jagged crystals.

Based on these results, can you imagine what *your* thoughts are doing to *you*? Since your body is ~70% water, you—your mind—has so much power over your wellbeing.

This means you can decide how you feel by:
- Being kind to yourself
- Choosing to think positively
- Choosing to override negative dialogue
- Hydrating your body optimally
- Providing your body with optimum levels of oxygen to get your *prana* flowing (the breathing exercises discussed earlier are a great tool for this)

Yes, it really is as simple as that. But it takes commitment to make these practices part of us and be mindful.

A few years ago, my husband got a new job and we had to move to another state halfway across the country. This necessitated a house hunt during the peak of summer in 90–105 degree heat. I would fly in for a weekend and our realtor and I would drive from one house to another—we saw almost 150 houses. It was my job to narrow down the possibilities to the top five, and then my husband and I were to finalize our selection together. I didn't find anything I liked from the houses that were available at the time in the community we desired the most, and unfortunately, we didn't find anything in our second community preference either.

Our schedule to see the homes was always packed since I was shuttling from state to state. We even set a record for our realtor—we saw 32 houses in one day. You are probably wondering how that is possible—actually, it was quite easy.

Some of the houses I didn't even enter. The conversation with our realtor went something like this…the realtor would park in front of the house and I would say, "Let's go and move on to the next house."

Realtor: "You liked the house online, it has everything you want—it's perfect for you."

Me: "The house has an invisible 'Do not enter' sign over it."

Realtor: With a confused look, "What do you mean?"

Me: "The house doesn't want me to come in."

Realtor: With an incredulous and exasperating look, "OK."

I felt bad for her because this is not how house hunting typically goes. But I told her to look on the bright side; we were covering a lot of ground quickly. There were many houses I would walk in and walk back out of without going any further than the foyer. By this time the realtor wasn't surprised at anything. In the houses I actually went into, the first thing I did was go to the center of the house, close my eyes, spread my arms and take a few deep breaths to feel the house:

- To sense its vibrations
- To feel if the house's vibrations were harmonious
- To feel whether the home had happy or unhappy impressions
- To feel if the land had positive vibrations
- To feel what the people living before had left in their vibration signatures   and how much work it would be to change, if needed
- To feel if the house wanted us there, if it would welcome us and give us shelter willingly

Since everything is energy, including our potential home and us, it was important for me to make sure we could all exist harmoniously for years to come.

In the end, there was only one house where I sat down on the back patio, closed my eyes and thought, *this feels right, this could be home.* At that point we bought the house even though it wasn't the right neighborhood for us, didn't have everything we wanted, was farther from work than my husband would have liked and was farther from the airport than we wanted. But it felt like home—because it had excellent vibrations. Now and then we all complain about some of the drawbacks, but we all agree it feels good to be at home.

That's how important vibrations are. Home should be a safe haven, a place where you feel welcomed not only by your family but also by the house itself. After all, we are energy too. On top of that, it affects us even more because our bodies are 70% water. Any energy thought that originates in our head or in the environment affects us. You may already be experiencing such feelings from time to time. For example, you may be prone to visiting certain friends over others, and prefer to meet other friends outside, even though you may be equally fond of them and they all live in nice places. In a room full of strangers you may be drawn to certain individuals, while you subconsciously may avoid others. There may be certain places that you are drawn to visit again and again, whereas you may avoid other places like the plague.... It is the vibrations of the place or an individual that you are responding to without consciously thinking about it.

We can definitely have full control over our thoughts. We can also have control over the choice of our environment. While we have no control over others' thoughts or actions, we do have complete control over how we react to them. By being positive and increasing our *prana* we raise our own personal vibration levels. We can also increase the vibrational level around us which influences others in our vicinity to be more positive.

Being positive makes it easier for us to be in the present and have better personal and professional lives:

- We enjoy better health
- People enjoy our company more and more
- Life looks good
- We feel more joyful
- Normal matters annoy us less
- We are more like an elephant, walking away from the barking/begging thoughts and not allowing

them to annoy us. Or ruling the sky like a hawk and soaring above the nuisances

- You are bigger than *the six-pronged mind—who, what, when, where why, and how*—because these are the tools given for you to rule, not be ruled

You now understand the importance and effect of positive thoughts and their effect on *prana*. You have felt the difference; you can choose to be a king—king of your thoughts and ruler of your thoughts, not a beggar.

Most music/singing/dancing affects us positively, because it raises our vibration levels and improves the vibrations of our surroundings, which helps everybody. Let us sing and see how you feel....

- Sing: sing anything...
- Now close your eyes and sing for a moment
- Notice yourself taking a deeper breath to sing, filling your lungs
- Feel the energy inside you moving in a circular motion upwards
- Notice how you forgot about everything but your song, and how it made you feel. Singing engages your whole being—your heart and mind get in sync and all the other thoughts leave—only the pleasure of singing remains which elevates your vibration levels, creating harmony within and around you.

Next time you are feeling low, sing—sing with passion or listen to classical/soothing music—immerse yourself in it and feel how you are being lifted, or dance—dance like no one is watching. Dance for yourself and immerse yourself in the dance so much so that only the dancing remains and not you.

One of my students (we will call him Edward) once asked me a very astute question as to how to stay positive or keep his vibration levels high when he is surrounded by negative thinking most of the day at work. Working in that kind of environment makes him cranky quickly and despite all his good intentions his defenses fall. His good intentions help, but are simply not enough.

I was very impressed by Edward's understanding of the situation and clarity of thinking. To gain a better understanding of his situation, I asked him what he does to help himself right now.

He said, "I brace myself for what is coming." And I probed, "Which is?" He replied, "Complaining, whining, blaming, back biting and reveling in the fall of others…to name a few things I experience every day. I find the lack of harmony very stressful. This kind of unreasonable behavior makes me angry."

I asked, "Why? And what do you do to keep yourself positive?"

He said, "I work hard at keeping myself positive. I do *pranayama* as you taught me. I do yoga, exercise, eat right, meditate and feel very peaceful until I have to deal with the constant nagging at work. I am fortunate my wife does not nag; rather she puts up with my complaining about people at work when I get home."

I asked, "How does your wife [also my student] react to your nagging? Does she get angry?"

He said, "She just listens, smiles, gives me a hug and says I am glad you are home, then smiles again and I forget about everything else."

Then I asked Edward, "If you are carrying a basket of beautiful flowers and someone wants you to exchange those lovely flowers for a basket of dirty, filthy, foul smelling, heavy stones, would you exchange it?"

He said, "NO! Why would I do that?"

I said, "I don't know why, but you are doing it."

He was perplexed at that and said, "No, that does not sound right. I have never done that."

I replied, "You do it every day at work." Edward remained confused.

The worst part of Edward's situation was the fear he felt of the onslaught of negativity every morning. The anticipation itself lowered his vibration frequency and lowered his positive defenses. He would be so afraid of the imminent misery that he suffered the consequences before he experienced the actual negativity at work, again when he experienced it, and once more after he experienced it because he would be so angry about it. Essentially, his vibration levels decreased every time he thought about it.

It is like paying your fully paid debt over and over again, and each time the penalty increases. Imagine that you have paid your credit card bill fully and are then paying the same bill again and again with interest in the same month, even though it was already fully paid to begin with. This probably seems quite unfair, but we do this all the time when we revisit old distresses—by reliving the experience and feeling the onslaught of the same negativity related to the issues, the suffering increases with the added force of not having let go. The same recurring bill costs you more. I have had the pleasure of being in such situations in the past.

Edward finally understood that by allowing his vibration levels to decrease as a result of thinking about the negative workplace environment, he was essentially exchanging his positive, lovely flowers for a basket of polluted stones. His vibration levels and attitude are actually in his control, and he can actively work to remain unaffected by others, and willingly share positive energy in the workplace.

Even though Edward practiced to keep his vibrations at a high frequency, he was unable to keep himself unaffected by others, because he was only concerned with himself. I explained to him that we do not live in a bubble, but in a society, where everyone's actions affect each other. However, we only have control over our own actions. No matter how much we want or need we cannot wish or force change on others. It is a part of evolution for all of us, and we all evolve differently at different times and rates. Just like different flowers blossom at different times of the year and at different rates. Even flowers on the same bush do not blossom at the same time or look identical. That is the beauty of life. Imagine if everything blossomed and grew at once in nature—it would be a disaster! We would have too much of everything in a very short amount of time for a very short time, that we would not be able to adequately harvest and store. It would go to waste and then we might starve, as nothing would blossom or grow again. The world would be a dreary, dull place.

To succeed in life we must learn to flow with life events

Edward and I talked about and practiced a few techniques for different situations to help him continue to maintain his own vibrations, and get a better understanding of himself so that he could be happy in most circumstances. He learned to stop "paying" for the negative situations that resulted in lowered vibration levels.

First, Edward learned to *not fear* the upcoming situation. This was possible only by accepting it. We cannot change anyone—people change only when they want to and for themselves. By *accepting* that it is how it is, Edward stopped his "first payment" resulting from fear of the situation.

Second, he armed himself with *awareness*. He started dealing with his coworkers with awareness which allowed him to leave their basket of stones with the coworkers; which was heavy for them, as well. One day, when they are ready, they too shall rid *themselves* of that basket of stones by raising their vibration levels.

Third, Edward *lost his anger* because he was not afraid and instead had compassion for his coworkers.

Fourth, he stopped *judging* his coworkers for things they had no control over, and instead developed the desire to help and share his basket of flowers.

Fifth, he *felt assured* with his new found awareness and worked with a smile because he was not angry at his coworkers for who they were and their actions. He was not judging them, as no one wants to be miserable and everyone wants to be happy. Everyone wants to be joyful as that is our natural state of being, but life happens.

Sixth, Edward became a *more likable* person. Even though he vibrated at a higher frequency, he was not necessarily liked by others. He had worked hard and raised his vibration levels, but he had not been able to accept his negative emotions. Rather he judged and criticized internally which caused him misery for the longest time. Once he accepted his coworkers at all three layers—physically, mentally and emotionally—he was truly accepting of them. They sensed the shift in his attitude and it reflected in their attitudes. For example, they started including him in their after-hours activities. This made Edward very happy as he had always felt left out.

Seventh, Edward always loved himself, but his acceptance of himself as he was, and moving into awareness, brought on the change of accepting others as they were. As a result, *love towards his coworkers* flowed easily from him, without any effort. He started looking forward to going to work and found joy in being with others, and even started helping them resolve their issues. He became a pebble in the pond with far and lasting effects around him.

You see, we can only give what we have. We may choose not to give, but we cannot give what we do not have. A seeing person can help a blind man cross the street, but a blind man cannot help anyone cross the street. You can give a ride to another person only if you have a vehicle. A person without a vehicle cannot give you a ride (they can pay for your cab/bus/train fare only if they have the means). We see examples of this in nature all around us—a tree gives shade from the sun and protection from rain, air gives us *prana* to breathe, the sun gives us its sunshine, rain makes us wet, snow makes us cold, the moon gives us its moonlight and so on. Similarly, an unhappy person has only sorrow to share and a happy person has joy to share. An understanding of this helps us to accept, rather than resent, others. We accept them and have patience that they will change only when they are ready, and then too for themselves and not for us. This is a big leap of understanding and it takes us farther along the road of joy.

Edward learned that humans will be humans. We are

an emotional species and will act according to how we feel, perceive and understand. He understood the importance and effect of positive thoughts and increased *prana*. He practices *pranayama* every day. He enjoys music and uses it to quickly change the vibrations of any place, and when he is by himself he even dances!

CHAPTER SEVEN

Love and Acceptance

"Happiness can exist only in acceptance." ~ George Orwell

All of us want to be happy. At times we find happiness to be slippery and difficult to hold on to—one moment you have it and the next moment it's gone. We seem to be forever chasing happiness. We chase peace, whether for ourselves, our loved ones or for the world, and we always think it's farther away than it actually is.

Have you heard the story of the rich merchant, his son and the quest for happiness? Once upon a time there was a wealthy merchant who lived with his parents, wife, son and daughter in a very beautiful house. Their house had elaborate grounds, with a small river flowing behind the house. That's where the family gathered in the evenings after the day's work when the chores were complete. The adults would sit and talk and catch up, and the children would play in the water, swim or run around with their friends and neighbors. They all enjoyed the beautiful, peaceful, happy existence without any worries.

As time passed, the children became young adults. The daughter of the family married and moved to her husband's home, and the father/merchant passed on the secrets of the trade and even the secret to happiness to his son, as was the custom. The son quickly mastered the tools of the trade and did very well. He had a knack for it and quadrupled his father's business in just a few years, and got married to a nice, young woman. He had more money than he had ever imagined possible. He and his wife lived lavishly and were powerful people in their town. He had power, money and prestige, but was not happy. He knew he was taught the secret to happiness but he couldn't remember it. His parents had passed away so there was no one to ask.

In an attempt to be happy he worked harder and harder, growing the business even more and working to expand to neighboring towns. He still found himself unhappy so he worked to build more prestige and more recognition for the family business. Despite all of this he continued to be unhappy, and wished to find the secret of happiness which he had forgotten. He would often reminisce about the carefree days of the past when he was happy, and talk about "the good old days" with his wife. She was a wise woman. One day she said to him, "You have gained a lot of material wealth since then, have married, and your parents have passed on but you are still the same person—when you figure out what has changed you might find the secret to happiness."

He liked the idea and began introspecting. After some time he figured it out. He realized that earlier he was very accepting of himself, but not so much in recent years. To make up for his lack of self-acceptance, he had been focused on amassing wealth and power, and sought to be recognized by others. He also understood that as nice as it is to have wealth and power, it did not fill the hole he had been feeling, which nothing could seemingly fill. He realized that to feel better about himself he would be critical of others. He figured out that he was happier with less when there was self-acceptance—because there was self-acceptance, there was love for self. With this revelation he remembered the secret to happiness:

Happiness lies within

A lack of acceptance of our circumstances and ourselves causes significant stress in our lives. A 2012 study by the American Psychological Association showed that excessive work stress could increase the risk of a heart attack. Those with demanding jobs were found to have a 23 percent higher risk of suffering from a heart attack.

According to this study, more than one in five Americans reports living with consistent extreme stress. Chronic stress has also been linked with an increased risk of diabetes, cancer and Alzheimer's disease, among other negative health consequences.

Most of the problems in life stem from a lack of acceptance—our actual state versus the desired state, i.e. seeing, wanting or desiring the circumstances to be something other than reality. Whether it is something simple or complicated—someone not listening and making us feel ignored and unwanted, being passed over for a promotion by a coworker who is not very good at the actual work, parents seemingly playing favorites between children, not getting the gift you really wanted for your birthday, or your local barista messing up your regular coffee order—unacceptance of reality results in unhappiness.

100% acceptance of yourself is the hardest thing you will ever achieve. Since you are reading these words that means, as hard as it may be, you are interested and up to the challenge.

A C C E P T: This six-letter word is such a beautiful word that sounds even better to the ears…. Say it out loud for me, "accept." Yes, once again, this time slowly – "A C C E P T." Acceptance is something we all want but are unable to give. You know what the saddest part of all of this is? We don't give full acceptance to ourselves. We are all guilty of partial acceptance at one time or another, even of ourselves.

Acceptance is easier said than done, of course, but it is definitely possible. There are usually some driving forces behind a lack of acceptance. The biggest ones are anger and fear.

Fear is paralyzing. Fear of an expected event is worse than the actual event itself, because we always imagine the worst.

Let me tell you a story from personal experience. A few years ago, I was travelling from one city to another, and waiting at the airport. A handsome young couple sat by me and we started chatting. They were expecting their first child. During our discussion I learned that they had successful careers, came from loving families and had a nice home in an affluent neighborhood. They should have been textbook happy, so I was intrigued to learn that they were very worried about the factor of smartness, not intelligence, of their expected child. To them the future of their child depended on the right school from preschool to high school, the right extracurricular activities, and then going to the right university. You get the picture. Their biggest worry was that they were on a waiting list for the admission of their child to the so-called "right preschool."

My heart went out to this lovely young couple, who on top of these future worries had also had a very difficul time getting pregnant. The pregnancy itself was complicated, and the worry wasn't helping this young woman, whom I will call Nancy.

I asked Nancy, "How are you feeling?"

She said, "Very stressed."

I asked, "About what?"

She replied, "Besides all the worries about my baby growing up in the right way, I am always afraid I might miscarry. I have already had two miscarriages. This was a difficult conception and I am so worried that my baby may not make it to full term."

My heart went out to Nancy as this is the worst fear for any mother-to-be. I asked her what she was doing to help herself. She replied, "Everything the doctors have asked me to do, from taking my prenatal vitamins to bed rest when needed."

I said, "That's wonderful, but what are you doing to calm your fears?"

She helplessly shrugged her shoulders.

After a little more discussion we collectively agreed on a plan for Nancy:

- Perform breathing exercises to feel calm
  - o As you breathe: follow your breath and feel it going to your womb and loving your baby
  - o Make sure you exhale fully so that carbon dioxide is exhaled and there is more room for oxygen, which we all need
- Accept that you are doing everything in your power to help your child
- Don't worry about what has not happened yet, as worry could cause it to happen

- Read to your unborn child. Read stories of love, courage, integrity, imagination, wonder and the value of truth
- Sing to your child

She had shared her contact information so we kept in touch and she continued to stick to the plan. She practiced her breathing and became more and more mindful of it. She remained on my radar after we departed, as I felt empathetic towards her—she is such a gentle soul carrying such a big burden, trying to have control where there was none to have. In due course, she had a healthy baby. She continues to practice breathing as it helps her stay calm and impart the same feeling to her child. She has become a secure and happy young woman and mother as the breathing exercises help her stay in the present. She once put it very succinctly, telling me, "I am very happy because all of my worries are ahead of me and I am too smart to chase them. I would rather enjoy my present." After hearing those words, I knew I did not need to worry about Nancy anymore as she had learned to live in the present.

People do not always realize that our emotions can, and do, affect our physical and mental health. According to the Centers for Disease Control and Prevention, up to 90% of all illness and disease may be stress–related. Negative thoughts are stressful and that affects our bodily functions. Our stress usually comes from lack of acceptance of our circumstances, when we wish things to be different and our energies are spent on resisting and resenting rather than dealing with the issue at hand. Life gets difficult at times and at times like that it helps to step back and take a breather and recharge yourself.

I remember in my twenties there were times when life

got to be too much, too many fires at the same time, and I experienced feelings of helplessness and anger. At times like that I would take time off to recuperate and call it a mental health day. In retrospect it was a good thing to take time out for myself for things I enjoyed. I remember going back to sleep after the children went to school, or out for a walk in the park by myself with a picnic lunch and sitting under a tree to eat and read. Little things that I felt deprived of doing in my otherwise daily grind. That unscheduled one day for myself did wonders for my mental health. I went back to work rejuvenated and was more refreshed at home with my family. In a manner of speaking, recharging your batteries is necessary. I was able to do it because I accepted the need for it and did not feel guilty skipping errands and house work.

One of my students, Sarah, is a lovely young lady—a beautiful, kind, giving human being who is wise beyond her years yet still innocent like a child. She was an academic and sports star in high school and won many awards and scholarships. A few years later in life she started having shoulder pain and foot pain. She saw many doctors, chiropractors and healers. After about a year of treatment, breathing and meditation, her pain decreased by almost 80%, to a level at which she could function normally. Like most young girls, Sarah is fond of wearing heels—something that continues to be difficult for her. She has other more serious health issues which she manages beautifully, but not being able to wear heels bothers her. It may seem trivial to us, but to her it is significant. We all have things that bother us, which may seem insignificant to others. How we feel is always of most importance, regardless of what others think. We matter—in fact, we matter the most—because that is the foundation of A C C E P T A N C E.

I share Sarah's story because part of her recovery was acceptance. I would often tell her to make friends with her pain. After a lot of resistance, she accepted it at a physical level, then she accepted it in her head and then finally, emotionally, which is the hardest part. Every time she starts to feel resentful her pain returns at a higher intensity. As soon as she accepts it, focuses her attention on the pain in her foot, takes a few deep breaths and sends loving energy, her pain instantly decreases and becomes milder.

Even after experiencing and going through this cycle again and again it will continue until Sarah let's go of *why*—*why* this is happening to her—and accepts the situation fully.

We cannot allow our mind to go rogue on us. It requires constant vigilance and the reminder that you are in charge. It happens slowly, but the mind does change and aids you in your transformation.

Usually our acceptance is conditional; it can be seen as temporary acceptance. For instance, if you don't like your GMAT, LSAT, tennis or golf score, etc. you will accept the outcome only until you have the chance to practice and improve. Temporary acceptance is very valuable in our lives; it allows and enables us to put the emotional weight of the event aside and work more earnestly to improve upon our previous performance.

You have achieved acceptance when you are able to accept yourself fully and unconditionally, and therefore, love yourself completely, embracing your strengths and weaknesses. Take roses for example—we love and admire them for their beauty, and accept thorns as part of the package. We expect, and accept, corn to have a husk, rice to grow in muddy fields and lotus flowers to grow in muddy water. So why not accept ourselves? Only with acceptance can unconditional love flow.

- *Love yourself* and love will flow from you
- *Accept yourself* and acceptance will flow from you
- *Accept life* as it comes and peace will flow towards you
- *Be open* to new experiences and wonder will flow towards you
- *Open your heart* to others and love will flow towards you
- *Accept yourself and others* and harmony will flow towards you

If you love and accept yourself just the way you are, completely, without any ifs or buts, then:

- You will gain peace
- You will gain friendships and the ability to forgive
- You will gain joy and happiness and live a stress free life
- You will be in better health
- You will gain confidence
- You will be secure in yourself
- You will lose anger
- You will lose judgment
- You will lose fear
- You will lose insecurity
- …

The universal truth is that we cannot truly love anyone until we love ourselves, or accept anyone until we accept ourselves. Most of the relationships in our lives have strings attached—there is an element of expectation, whether reasonable or unreasonable. This will vary depending on the mental state of the person you love. This same person might react differently to the same scenario depending on how he or she is feeling towards themselves at that time. We have all experienced it.

Why do we wait for the right moment to ask for a favor from others or make our pitch in the boardroom? We want to catch the person granting a favor in the right mood or frame of mind. Children seem to have it just right; they have an uncanny ability to ask in the perfect way, the right parent and at just the right time.

When I was a child, I thought I excelled at this skill. My grandmother would tell my father, "Your daughter has figured you out better than me and you give her everything she wants." What I didn't know then was that my father, a wise man, was well aware of my tactics and was teaching me to negotiate by allowing me to think I had succeeded and making it harder each time thereafter, forcing me to make a better, more convincing and polished argument, and become adept at communication and have clarity of thought. It forced me to understand what I wanted, why I wanted it, if it was important enough to fight for, what it was going to do for me and how to convince others to give it to me. My father was a high ranking officer in a governmental organization. Even today, when I make my pitch to him, if I can convince him I know I can convince anyone.

When we had children, my husband and I decided to use

the same principle or psychology in raising our girls. Our first born is a straightforward, logical and intelligent child, and expected the logic and fairness of a situation to work. But that's not how the world works. Understanding and accepting that, we decided to teach her to negotiate. We would say a soft "no" to things that were perfectly reasonable. She would get hurt and angry and say, "You are not fair." I would tell her, "You are right, fight for your rights, don't give in," and she would reply, "What can I do? You are my parents there is nothing I can do." I would tell her to negotiate, and she began to do so slowly and gradually. We made it easy for her at first, and then more and more complex. Today she is a successful consultant and negotiates all the time. The gentle soul that she is, her expectation is still for life to be fair, but she accepts that it isn't and negotiates fairly without taking undue advantage.

Until the age of ten, I went to my grandfather for emotional support or extra money, knowing that he would listen patiently without judgement and then buy me an ice cream—and my world would be perfect again. Similarly, for something new I would go to my father, for help with school I went to my mother, and I didn't go to my grandmother for anything because I had learned from experience that she would ask too many questions and after interrogating me would send me away. I am sure this sounds familiar…we all have our go-to people.

My choice of go-to people kept changing as I got older but the concept stayed the same. In my teens, my friends were my source of emotional support and my parents and brother were my source for unconditional love and acceptance (and of course financial needs). Today, I go to my husband and children for love, understanding and friendship; my mother for acceptance and emotional support; my father for wisdom; my brother and his wife for help and support; and my Guru for unconditional love, guidance, friendship and acceptance. Everyone I know comes to me for unconditional love and acceptance, because I have self-acceptance and love for myself and that is what they expect.

This support system is very important. We are very fortunate if we receive unconditional love—we do not need it from everybody. To be loved for who and what we are, even from one person, is enough. This could come from a parent, friend, sibling, significant other, pet, or even nature. Receiving unconditional love aids us in loving ourselves in the same fashion.

In acceptance there is no conflict and the mind is calm

Love and Acceptance go hand in hand. You cannot love anyone for too long without accepting them for who they are, and love will always follow acceptance.

Baba, my Guru, would often say, "Real love resides within you and there is nowhere to go but within, where there exists an ocean of love waiting for you." Then he would laugh and say, "Rise in love my child, rise in love." That would really leave me perplexed, as I had only heard of falling in love.

I conducted a survey of individuals in an attempt to decipher "rise in love." The survey had three main questions:

1. What does love mean to you? (a few interesting responses below)

2. Have you ever been in love?

3. Have you ever risen in love?

"*When you want to do something for others without any expectations*"

"*Love is feeling a flutter, like being on cloud nine*"

"*Love is easy, having someone to hold and hug you and make you feel cared for. Love is having someone to share your day and both good and bad moments with*"

"*Love is when mommy lets me eat all the ice cream I want*"

"*Love is a beautiful feeling that brings out the best in you, when you are in love you are in love with the universe...you don't remain yourself...you just melt like snow and flow like a river into the ocean*"

"*True love is selfless...in selflessness you become LOVE itself*"

"*Love is feeling a high all the time*"

"*When I am in love I don't mind criticism*"

"*Love cannot be defined*"

"*Love is compassion for all living beings*"

"*Love is lending a helping hand without any expectations*"

"*There is no expiration date to love*"

"*When I am in love I have this goofy smile on my face all the time*"

"*Love is surrender*"

"*The world looks so beautiful when in love*"

"*When in love I feel invincible*"

To my second question, "Have you ever been in love?" 90% of participants responded with *yes*, and interestingly, most of the participants' interpretation of love was romantically inclined. Very few linked it with love of nature, family, universe, friends, pets.... The answer to my third question was a question back, asking me, "What is rising in love?" and discussions on falling in love and its disappointments. Participants talked about their loves—most people ended with an "until you fall out of love" statement and then anger, guilt, and resentment took over. I asked if they believed they could rise in love and always be on cloud nine, that they would always be loved back unconditionally? You guessed it, no one believed me, and rightly so.

The kind of love we understand usually relates to our acceptance by others without judgment, while we constantly judge ourselves and others. That love is only as deep as our skin. Tell me, is it fair to expect something from others that we do not give ourselves? This is something we could give, but we don't. At times our love for ourselves is also skin deep.

As we talked about in the "Power of Breath" chapter, *Prana* is life force energy. It is that *Prana* that makes our heart beat and makes us alive. The amazing reality is that *Prana* is the same in everyone, in every species and in every race. It is that very special part of you that is hidden by several layers of conditioning by society. Find that part of yourself and go deeper than the skin.

We have been taught from childhood to associate ourselves with our physical bodies—the needs of our physical bodies, the relation of our body's successes, the name and titles given to our physical body and the possessions of our gross (physical) body. We introduce ourselves in the same fashion; for example, Oprah Winfrey may say, "I am Oprah Winfrey, media proprietor, talk show host, philanthropist, actress…" or Melinda Gates may say, "I am Melinda Gates, Co-chair of the Bill & Melinda Gates Foundation and wife of Bill Gates..." However, if you ask an enlightened soul, he or she would say, "I am the same as you," or he or she might say, "I am Divine, just like you."

If I asked one of my friends to introduce herself she would have said something like this: "Hi, my name is Michelle. I am a pilot. I am married to a school teacher and have two children. I play the piano, like old movies, enjoy cooking, have many friends," and so on. However, a couple of years ago she did not wake up—her heart had stopped in her sleep. She was still there physically, but not actually there as there was no life force energy, no *Prana*, no life that made her alive.

It was one of the most difficult days of my life, as I sat trying to help my friend's family go through the process of acceptance and understand that Michelle is more than what they thought her to be. Over many weeks and months the family finally understood the concept. Now every time Michelle's name is mentioned they have a big smile and her children reiterate that we are more than our body. They are a lovely family—I am thankful to them for allowing me to be part of their family and being open to the idea that there is more to life than what meets the eye.

I agree that our physical body is very important and necessary to survive in this world, because that is how we exist physically and that is how people identify us. I am simply asking you to realize and accept that you are more than what is obvious. I repeat, go deeper than your skin and find that special part of you.

Allow me to share another story:

When God created the world (per common belief),

everything was going well. In those days God used to live on the earth. He created the trees, the flowers, the mountains, the rivers, etc. But why did he create them? The story says that he created them to live in, to be here.

Then he created man, and something went awry. With the creation of man, trouble began as man started complaining. Whenever something went wrong man did not care if it was morning or midnight or whether God was asleep or not. Man would come and knock on God's door with his complaints.

So God asked his Angels, "What should I do?" One of them suggested, "You better go to the Himalayas and hide there." God replied, "You are right, that makes sense. But you don't know the future, sooner or later a man named Edmund Hillary will come to Mount Everest. They will not leave me alone even there."

So they said, "It would be good if you go to the moon." God replied, "No, it will help for just a little while but then man is going to reach everywhere."

Then one old Angel whispered something in God's ear, and God nodded and said, "Yes, you are right."

Can you guess what that old Angel said to God?

He said: "Better you hide yourself in man himself. Go deep into his heart and hide yourself there." God replied, "You are right because he will never suspect to look for me there."

All you have to do is understand your real self, that something which makes you alive—that life force energy, that light within all of us, that ocean of love in all of us. With acceptance you start your journey to yourself. By loving your real self, you "rise in love." Your real self is pure, perfect and unconditionally loving and accepting. It took me some time, but I finally understood what my Guru meant when he told me to "rise in love." He was teaching me that when we "fall in love" we may subconsciously become disempowered and codependent, whereas "rising in love" is the purest form of love. It becomes the state of your being and you yourself become love—love is the natural state of your being. Mahatma Gandhi once said, "Where there is love there is life." How can one celebrate life without love—unconditional love? Just as the sun loves the earth and every one of us on it, without any discrimination of gender, race, socioeconomic standing, nationality, profession, age or appearance. It quietly shines on the whole earth. As the poet Rumi put it...

"And still after all this time, the Sun has never said to Earth,
'You owe me.'
Look what happens with love like that.
It lights up the sky." ~Rumi

We have intellect to help guide us towards that source of unlimited love stemming from our core. We also have the Mind which prefers to be in charge. Instead of serving us it would rather rule us like so many of our modern devices. Our Mind loves these devices and keeps us entertained and up to date. Like Apps on our smart phones, we have an App for gaining control of our Mind too—*Pranayama,* as discussed in "Power of Breath." It is built in, and came with our hardware—with some fine tuning it can and will take you to self-acceptance.

I am hoping you are ready to commit to the most important commitment of your life—loving and accepting yourself and others without judgment. In doing so, the feelings of anger, fear, guilt, comparison, jealousy and resentment will be replaced by a wonderful feeling of happiness and joy.

Love is giving, sharing, and accepting without interference from mind across all three layers—Mind, Heart and Body. This will be further discussed in the "Three Layers" chapter. Where there is acceptance, there is love. As you love yourself, your real self, you will love everything and everyone else as they all have the same life force.

I say to you what my Guru often said to me when I would get angry or frustrated because I was judging myself or others: "Be like the SUN. Give love without any strings attached and you will have no reason to be upset." One of the most important life lessons....

Remember, love is beyond the mind

I would like to share a composition I came across. The origin of these lines is uncertain, however, some people believe it to be a speech given by Charlie Chaplin on his 70th birthday.

<u>As I Began To Love Myself</u>

As I began to love myself I found that anguish and emotional suffering are only warning signs that I was living against my own truth. Today, I know, this is **AUTHENTICITY.**

As I began to love myself I understood how much it can offend somebody as I try to force my desires on this person, even though I knew the time was not right and the person was not ready for it, and even though this person was me. Today I call it **RESPECT.**

As I began to love myself I stopped craving for a different life, and I could see that everything that surrounded me was inviting me to grow. Today I call it **MATURITY**.

As I began to love myself I understood that at any circumstance, I am in the right place at the right time, and everything happens at the exactly right moment. So I could be calm. Today I call it **SELF-CONFIDENCE**.

As I began to love myself I quit stealing my own time, and I stopped designing huge projects for the future. Today, I only do what brings me joy and happiness, things I love to do and that make my heart cheer, and I do them in my own way and in my own rhythm. Today I call it **SIMPLICITY**.

As I began to love myself I freed myself of anything that is no good for my health—food, people, things, situations, and everything that drew me down and away from myself. At first I called this attitude a healthy egoism. Today I know it is **LOVE OF ONESELF**.

As I began to love myself I quit trying to always be right, and ever since I was wrong less of the time. Today I discovered that is **MODESTY**.

As I began to love myself I refused to go on living in the past and worry about the future. Now, I only live for the moment, where EVERYTHING is happening. Today I live each day, day by day, and I call it **FULFILLMENT**.

As I began to love myself I recognized that my mind can disturb me and it can make me sick. But as I connected it to my heart, my mind became a valuable ally. Today I call this connection **WISDOM OF THE HEART**.

We no longer need to fear arguments, confrontations or any kind of problems with ourselves or others. Even stars collide, and out of their crashing new worlds are born. Today I know **THAT IS LIFE!**

CHAPTER EIGHT

Three Layers

"A man is but the product of his thoughts—what he thinks he becomes." ~ Mahatma Gandhi

The most powerful energy in this universe is thought. A single pointed thought has taken a man to enlightenment and a single pointed thought has taken a man to the path of destruction, as well. The thoughts or images that run through our mind trigger a response from our body, as well as our heart. If the thought is strong it will impact our feelings and body, resulting in action.

One day I was passing by a bakery and it triggered a memory. The memory of the rum carrot cake my friend Pam used to make for us. The cake was not only a culinary memory; it was a memory of a friend's love that had passed. The memory was so intense that it was painful. I could see Pam in my memory, giving me a slice with a twinkle in her eyes; I could taste the cake in my mouth, feel the perfect balance of textures, nuts, raisins and carrots; could smell the nutmeg and cinnamon and kick of rum. I suddenly realized that my mouth was watering and I had to have a piece of rum carrot cake. So much so, that I called a few specialty restaurants and bakeries to find a rum carrot cake. They had carrot cake, but not rum carrot cake. The desire to eat that rum carrot cake was so strong that I searched online for a good carrot cake recipe, went to the grocery store to buy all the ingredients, including rum, came home and baked the cake the same day. Once it was done I called a few of my friends over and we celebrated Pam with rum carrot cake. Talk about the power of a thought! It had me salivating for the comfort of friends and rum carrot cake. It felt good to translate a positive nurturing memory into an equally beautiful heartfelt physical experience.

My Guru often said, "Most things we do in life involve at least three layers of our being: Mind – Heart – Body." He would further tie it to karma/action and warn us to be forever watchful of our thoughts and feelings.

At first that did not make any sense to me, because doing was just doing to me. How I felt about the job at hand did not change the fact that it had to be done. If I needed to clean the house, I had to clean the house. If I needed to cook, well, then I needed to cook. If I needed to pick the kids up from school, I had to pick them up. I did not have much choice in the matter. Yes, I will admit, if I did my chores joyfully it was a pleasant experience for me and the people around me. Once I became aware of how my attitude is affecting people around me, I became mindful. I started doing the most mundane jobs with mindfulness. I would think of my Guru's words before starting any chore, and I would take a deep breath and tell myself, "You are going to do this task and spend time and energy on it, so do it joyfully—that way you are happy doing it and keeping your environment vibrating positively at a higher level."

The body follows the cues from our mind and heart. The result of anything we do is directly related to how we feel at that moment. Take, for example, something as simple as cooking. When you cook from the heart, your mind and body follow and the result is spectacular food. One of my students does not like to cook at all. However, at times, not cooking is not an option. During our discussions one day, I told her to involve her heart in the process and change the environment of cooking. She said, "What do you mean? Cooking is cooking and I do not like it." I replied, "I understand. Nonetheless, since you have no choice in the matter, why don't you experiment with a few changes?" So we agreed on a plan.

Before stepping into the kitchen, she would:

- Put on her favorite music
- Take three nice, deep cleansing breaths
- Pour herself a glass of wine

Once the atmosphere was that of relaxation and fun, she could step into the kitchen and:

- Cook a simple meal
- Clean up after cooking, and finally
- Go back to the living room and evaluate the experience

We agreed that she would stick to the plan and then talk to me after a week. I am happy to report that our plan worked—I still remember the excitement in her voice when she called and said, "It was amazing. I did not know cooking could be fun. My husband was amazed and even cleaned up after dinner. I can do this on a regular basis. It was nice to eat at home rather than eating out all the time. My husband and I are even cooking together now and finding new recipes to try. Even when I am just cooking a meal for myself, it is nice to finally enjoy the process."

The explanation behind this transformation is really quite simple. Music changed the vibrations of both my student and her environment, and affected her mind and heart, sending cues of peace and harmony. The glass of wine was an indulgence, and cooking became a labor of love instead of a dreaded chore. It was the same chore as before, but her outlook had changed as her emotions were positive and as a result, her mental outlook became positive, as well.

Our thoughts influence our emotions and actions but our emotions and actions also influence our thoughts. All three layers of our being are used in anything we do—from walking in the park to presenting in a board room—whether we are aware of it or not. We use our mind for logistics/thinking, our heart/emotions act as a gauge for how much effort to put into the job and our body is also affected by the intensity of thought behind it, and in turn the mind is again stimulated. Your awareness of your thoughts and emotions will influence the outcome of everything you do, from work to cooking to sex to friendships to relationships and everything in between. The sooner we are aware that our every thought has a reaction, the sooner we can work towards making it a reaction we want—a positive outcome. By being more aware of our thoughts and emotions, we also accumulate good Karma.

Almost all successful people have one thing in common—they are 100% completely committed to their work—mind, heart and body. They have a burning desire to succeed where they are and work towards their goal. Since the commitment is there, all of their mental, physical and emotional energy is devoted to a single goal. In this situation, the universe also works with them. It is simple science—thought is energy which is vibration, and if that vibration has emotions attached, the intensity is even greater, and the greater the intensity, the greater the results.

Scientists tend to work tirelessly with one, and only one, focus. A good bus driver drives a bus with the single focus of taking passengers safely from point A to B. A good office manager works with a goal to run the office efficiently. An athlete participates in a marathon to cross the finish line. A software programmer is focused on developing the next big thing. The Alpine ibex goats in Italy focus on climbing the steep walls of a brick dam for the salt on the stones without any care of falling. A politician is focused on getting the votes and winning. A student works hard for the best possible grades. A social reformer is focused on change. A yogi works towards self-realization. Each individual is as successful as their commitment to their goal.

Think of successful people you know—at work, in your family, in your social network. Someone you admire for their success. They are using their energy towards that success, at all the three layers:

- <u>Mentally</u>: they are constantly thinking about what they are trying to achieve, planning ways to reach their goal
- <u>Emotionally</u>: their heart is intensely focused on the object/goal and everything becomes secondary to the goal
- <u>Physically</u>: the body follows the mind and heart and they put in long hours relishing the thought of achieving their end goal

Do you think any president could win an election if they were not completely, single mindedly focused, and surrounded by a like-minded team? Do you think any athlete could compete in the Olympics? Do you think a child could take his first step if he was not fully focused: mind, heart and body? That is the way of life—at times we may be ruled by mind and at other times by heart. It takes being mindful to strike a balance.

I read these words a long time ago, and have them on a message board in my office:

"Watch your thoughts, they become your words;
Watch your words, they become your actions;
Watch your actions, they become your habits;
Watch your habits, they become your character;
Watch your character, it becomes your destiny."

~Unknown

It is the same with the love. All the famous love stories in history, people we know and admire who are in love even after 40-50-60-70 years, they are all committed to their love at all three layers—mind, heart and body.

Think about some of the broken relationships you see around you, and take a moment to ponder these questions:

- Are the people in that relationship mentally compatible and committed?
- Is there commitment at a physical level?
- Does the relationship have emotional focus and commitment?

Most likely, the answer to at least one of the above questions is *no*.

This concept of three layers applies to most activities in

life. For example, if you go to the gym to exercise, a trainer would tell you to visualize the results you want while pushing your body and heart to new limits. If you are focused on achieving a certain body image, then a similar concept also applies. Another example: if you're learning how to cook, a chef may tell you to engage with the food on multiple sensory levels and imagine what the end product should look like.

Food is essential for the sustenance of life—right? Most of us enjoy fruits, and I have randomly picked blueberries for demonstration:

Can you tell me what a blueberry really tastes like? When you put one in your mouth:

- Do you taste and feel the break of the skin under your teeth?
- Do you taste the grainy, sweet/tart mix of its pulp spread in your mouth?
- Do you feel the one hard part where it was attached to the stem?
- Do you feel some of the skin stuck in your teeth?
- Do you feel the satisfaction of eating refreshing fruit?
- Do you feel the release of antioxidants helping your body?
- Do you feel grateful to Mother Nature for providing this wonderful fruit?

If you focus with your mind, body and heart you can feel all the above and more! If you are eating and experiencing across the three layers, your mouth and taste buds will taste all the nuances of flavor and texture, your mind will notice you tasting and your heart will rejoice. This applies for any food.

I would like you to take a moment and experiment yourself—get a glass of water, take a deep breath, open yourself at all three layers and drink:

- Do you feel the wetness as the water goes into your mouth?
- Do you feel it going down your throat through the esophagus to the stomach?
- Do you feel the temperature of the water?
- Do you feel it quench your thirst? Or maybe not?
- How does it feel in your mouth and on your tongue?
- Do you feel thankful that fresh water is available to you so easily?
- Did you ever think drinking a glass of water could be so wonderful?

After conducting this experiment, most people find more pleasure and satisfaction from that same glass of water.

Maybe next time you eat your favorite fruit you can try this experiment.

- Get any piece of fruit from your kitchen. Wash it if it needs to be washed, and as you wash it feel the skin of the fruit and its texture. Then dry the fruit
- Take a deep abdominal breath
- Take two more of these wonderful deep breaths and feel yourself in the present moment

- Take a small bite and experience the wonder of it…

After you have experienced eating the fruit at all three layers, write a few lines describing your experience below:

_____
_____
_____
_____
_____
_____
_____
_____
_____
_____

Now that you have experienced the joy of engaging at all three layers when eating, you may find yourself wanting to experiment tasting everything in the same fashion. Be prepared to be amazed by the flavors in your cooking. You will notice the difference in fresh and frozen foods, and you will also notice the difference with processed foods.

I am excited at the thought of you tasting everything in a leisurely fashion, allowing your taste buds to explore and enjoying your meal at a whole new level. Similarly, you will find success following you when you do your work/projects at all three layers. Most importantly you will find joy in whatever you do. Anything done with love leads to spectacular results.

Enjoy operating at all three layers and remember to breathe deeply as you do.

We may not experience most things in life at all three layers, but we usually excel in engaging at all three layers when it comes to anger. When we are angry, our body is in use, whether just the tongue or more, and our mind is running and completely absorbed in the event. So much so that it often wants to stay engaged even after the event is over. Our heart and our emotions are participating fully along with mind and body, and we experience stress levels that can range from an increase in blood pressure to a heart attack.

Anger hurts the vessel it is stored in (that would be us) more than anybody else

Anger can feel like a best friend. The feeling of being wronged and needing the wrong to be righted. That simmering, seemingly justifiable feeling—our six-pronged mind wanting answers to *who, what, when, where, why* and *how* can be, and often is, all-consuming; leading our emotions to affect our own health adversely. While we feel this anger so deeply, it often has no effect on the other individuals or circumstances involved, the circumstances we have a hard time accepting. Our anger affects us the most and we often end up hurting innocent bystanders—especially, our loved ones. Yet we hold on to our anger and our grudges tightly, like a best friend.

Anger can stick to us like crazy glue. We pay this huge emotional price over and over again, and our body gets battered in the process. At times our need for justice and explanations keeps the flame of anger burning. When we finally decide that enough is enough, and use our intellect to help ourselves and accept circumstances as they are, only then are we able to move forward.

We have all probably been the victim of anger many times. Sometimes our hurt is so deep it is hard to let go. It is precisely at those times that it is of utmost importance to let go and make peace at all layers. We start by self-talk, that it is what it is and it is better to accept how it is. Then you get your mind on board. Once the mind is on board, emotions will also settle accordingly—you will feel more positive and your overall outlook improves and raises your vibration level, which, in turn, has a tremendous positive effect on your physical health.

We all feel and react to stress differently. An excessive amount of stress usually contributes to various health problems, such as high blood pressure, hives, asthma, ulcers, irritable bowel syndrome, even heart attacks and sudden death. Your body's response to stress may be anything from a headache to unexplained stomach pains to back strain. Stress can, and does, interfere with your sleep, and zap your energy and strength, making you cranky and preventing you from functioning at optimum levels or experiencing joy.

When one is stressed, one feels like a candle burning from both ends with nowhere to go. A feeling of being helpless and trapped takes over. I say that from experience. In my early thirties I felt the most stressed in my life. My husband and I both had good jobs that we enjoyed, we were blessed with two beautiful children who were the joys of our life, and lived in a nice house and drove nice cars—a typical middle class family. On the surface I had no reason to be stressed. I had everything I had worked towards or wanted, but I was not happy and was stretched too thin.

I carved time out for my husband, sharing his dreams, being a partner in his life at work and at home. He was also always available for the kids and helped me with the housework. I say it again, I had everything, yet I was sick all the time. I had unexplained severe headaches and stomach pain most of the time. I saw more specialists than I care to count. I could not keep food down and felt weak, nauseated and frustrated. I went from one doctor to another, and then I would get upset with them for not being able to figure out what was wrong with me and fix it. I had everything but my mind could not be still to appreciate my blessings. It did not know how to live in the present, only in the past or future, regret or future anticipation. I had completely forgotten that the mind was supposed to serve me, not the other way around.

Once I had to go to the ER while we were on vacation in San Francisco because I had severe stomach pain and nausea, pain that was beyond my tolerance. I was doubling over in pain and doctors had to give me something intravenously for quick relief. In the hospital they did several tests but didn't find anything.

Going to the ER while on vacation was scary for me and the children, so when we returned home I went to see a gastroenterologist. After conducting every uncomfortable test possible for my whole digestive system, he called me in for a half hour consultation. Until today I remember what he looked like—a man in his late fifties or early sixties, with silver grey hair and very kind eyes. He talked to me about my life and after few minutes told me I had irritable bowel syndrome. He also very gently told me that I needed to take better care of myself, and gave me a little handbook to read about how to reduce stress in my life, which was not nearly enough information as to how it would be possible.

I am thankful to the physician for the diagnosis and pointing me in the right direction, but I was on my own after that. It is like when we tell our children to "study hard"— that statement is just a statement until we provide them with the tools they need. In this case I was miserable enough to introspect and make much needed changes in my lifestyle.

Hindsight is always 20-20; hence, it is not surprising that now I see some of my life experiences in a different light. For instance, I now know the reasons for my misery in the past— my lack of acceptance and never-ending desires, whether for success, power or peace.

- My mind would race from topic to topic; I didn't take charge and focused on the past (what I had) and future (what I wanted or where I wanted to be).

- I was often caught up in the *who, what, when, where, why* and *how* of events, but never enjoyed the moment.

- I seldom felt peaceful, as my mind took control of every situation, event and relationship. I lived my life with my mind, not heart. My mind was happy when busy and didn't let me live in the moment. I spent much of my time immersed in emotions such as envy, fear, and anger.

- When I did feel happiness, there was an attached fear of losing it, which put too much pressure on being happy.

- Moments of success were tied to materialistic achievements. The mind was excited by my house, my car, my job, my trinkets, my x, my y, my z—you get the picture.

In airplanes, before the flight is airborne, the flight attendants go over the safety procedures, emergency exits and how to operate oxygen masks. We are told to put our own oxygen mask on before trying to help anyone else, even our own child. For good reason: if we neglect to put our mask on and start helping others, we might become incapacitated and be in no condition to help; the other person is put at risk too. Whereas, if we put our mask on first and are able to breath, then we would be in good shape to help others.

Looking back now with more experienced eyes, I can appreciate the importance of putting on my own oxygen mask first. During that period of my life I did not put on my oxygen mask first, and kept giving to everyone and thus, became incapacitated. In other words, I did not pay attention to my own needs. It was a defining moment in my life. I started carving time out for myself. I got back into yoga and started doing my breathing exercises again. I got back in touch with my friends and did things to please myself. Putting my oxygen mask on first resulted in more energy, and I was able to spend time with myself without sacrificing time with my children or my husband, and everyone was happier because I was happier and healthier. Since then no matter how many demands life has of me I do not sacrifice my daily practice of *pranayama* and meditation—after all, those nerves need a workout too.

I emphasize to all my students that the less time you have, the more you need to be diligent about your breathing/ *pranayama* exercises and be mindful of your breath. It allows you to be an elephant and keep the barking dogs at bay. It helps keep your vibration level high and helps you to use your time efficiently without undue stress on you or others around you.

In fact, if you are not free from negative thought attacks, the after effects of the emotions continue to be visible on our body long after the event is over. I know some people who can, and do, hold grudges for decades. Each time they revisit the event, they relive the emotional trauma and every time the body and mind suffer. So why hold on to it? Emotional trauma is a gift that keeps giving until you break the cycle. How do we break the cycle? The good news is all you need is yourself and the willingness to let it go at all three layers.

I understand that some emotional issues are very painful and hard to forgive. I argue it is even more painful to hold on to them. Every time you hurt yourself all over again and suffer all over again, and your anger gets more and more rooted because you cannot believe that, after all this time the event has the power to hurt you again. Actually, that event has only as much power as you give it. Yes, you understood correctly:

- *The event is just an event, until you give it energy*
- You give it a hold over you
- You give it power
- And you can take it away

One of my students (I will call her Kate) got divorced a few years ago. It was one of the most painful times for me because I had to witness this wonderful child's suffering—suffering that she did not deserve. She is one of the most giving and self-sacrificing people I know. Not only is she beautiful inside and out, but also kind, intelligent, generous to a fault and successful, a rare combination of beauty, intellect and humility. She married her now ex-husband (Bob) for love, thinking that he loved her back. She loved the man selflessly but he was selfish and gave her a very hard time. He tried to rob her of her self-esteem and self-confidence as he was covering for his own low self-esteem and self-confidence. He even managed to swindle a bundle of money from her.

When Kate came to me, she was hurt, angry, bitter and full of "Why did it happen to me? What did I do wrong? If only I had not married him, how could he do this to me? How could I have been so stupid, it is not fair, I hate him, his family [because she expected them to behave better] and everybody else"—all very normal emotions given the circumstances.

The first thing we worked on was giving Bob a new name. We called him Good Riddance. It was a powerful suggestion for the brain to associate positive feeling with the divorce. Good Riddance.

Second, we worked on acceptance of how she felt. In time, she accepted the fact that she was cheated and that he was a mistake in her life, which she has paid for, without analyzing it or attaching any emotion to it. She was determined not to let him hurt her anymore, and acceptance helped her to not view herself as the victim. This is not an easy thing to do for anyone because every time the emotion surfaced she had to be in charge, instead of her mind/emotions. She continues to practice *pranayama* and awareness which has helped her maintain a positive frame of mind.

Third, I encouraged Kate to give some kind of symbolic farewell to that part of her life. We decided to have a bonfire and burn everything the young man stood for. She collected all the mementos and gifts, the marriage license, pictures with him and his family, wedding albums—everything that was associated with him. She even bought a little stuffed weasel and said, "This stands for him." She said all that she needed to say to that stuffed animal so that all the negative emotions were out of her and transferred to that poor stuffed weasel, and threw it in the bonfire along with everything else. With good riddance, she signified that that part of life was over and behind her. Then Kate and I opened a bottle of champagne and sipped the fine bubbly, letting go of things and releasing the hurt and pain. Simultaneously, Kate took back the power, and this helped her feel in charge and not a victim. Every now and then when emotions from the past resurface she reminds herself gently that she burned that part of her life and has let go. She takes a deep breath and becomes vigilant of her thoughts, says a small prayer of thanks for her blessings in life and goes about enjoying them. Kate has learned that it helps to accept life as it is, gracefully, at all three layers, because we cannot change it, only how we react to it.

> *The only thing we have control over is ourselves, and, that is enough. That is all you need.*

The following cleansing meditation exercise will help you let go of anger and unwanted emotions, and transition to a feeling of calmness and peace.

Cleansing meditation exercise:

Remember to let go with your mind, heart, body—all three layers—for the maximum benefit.

After reading the guidelines below, find a comfortable place to sit or lie down. Make sure you are wearing comfortable clothing.

- Sit with your spine straight, feet touching the floor gently
- Place hands on your knees
- Relax your shoulders
- If lying down, keep legs shoulder width apart, arms by your side palms down and feel the

surface under your body

- Close your eyes and observe yourself
- Feel the chair under your hips
- Feel the floor under your feet
- Feel the weight of your hands on your knees
- Take a deep breath—as you breathe in visualize the life force energy going into your body and spreading everywhere from head to toe
- Hold the inhale for a few seconds and enjoy this sensation of fullness
- Exhale and visualize as you press your stomach muscles against your ribs. Your lungs are releasing CO_2 and your body/nerves are releasing toxins, and they are leaving your body in each exhale
- Hold your exhale—even for a second—and savor this empty feeling.
- Take a deep breath—as you breathe in visualize the life force energy going into your body and spreading everywhere from head to toe
- Hold the inhale for a few seconds and enjoy this sensation of fullness
- Exhale slowly and visualize negative unwanted thoughts leaving your body like a grey sludge. Be mindful to let go of the hurt from your mind and heart so that your body can heal
- Then start the cycle of breathing again— inhale life force energy—hold—exhale what is not needed/wanted—hold—inhale life force energy…

Repeat 7-9 times or keep going, there is no need to count

- Take a deep breath—as you breathe in visualize the life force energy going in your body and spreading everywhere from head to toe
- Hold the inhale for a few seconds and enjoy this sensation of fullness
- Exhale and sense your body and heart feeling freer and lighter
- Stay with that feeling with your eyes closed for as long as you like…

It would be of great benefit to you to write down a few lines about how wonderful you feel after this cleansing meditation exercise. It is great to do this exercise a few times before going to bed or as soon as you come home. It will help you cleanse yourself of the emotional grime from the day, leaving you free to enjoy your evening and have a restful night.

"You can only adjust your sails, not the wind." ~Unknown

This breathing exercise gives you the strength to adjust your sails to move forward, allowing you to move from the vantage point of strength, no matter what…

CHAPTER NINE

The Mind

"Sometimes the chains that prevent us from being free are more mental than physical." ~ Evan Carmichael

Growing up I would wonder about the Mind. Is it the grey matter in my brain? Is it my Mind which thinks for me, reasons for me, experiences for me and feels for me? Is it my Mind that remembers, perceives, judges, discovers and loves? These thoughts did not please me as I did not like being ruled by my Mind—what if it was wrong? After all, it knows less than those who have been around longer than me, studied more than me or had more experience than me. Then the big question—is the Mind the same as intellect? Where is intellect located? What about wisdom? Where does that come from? Is that also a physical part of my body? I have seen very smart people being stupid, so being smart and wise must be two different things. These are some of the first questions I asked my Guru. He said, "Mind is a double edged sword. It can make your life heaven or hell; it can make heaven of hell and hell of heaven." Then he smiled his mischievous smile and said, "Use your intellect to figure it out."

Mind is a wonderful tool, an essential tool. Without its cooperation life would be difficult. Society teaches us from the beginning to take care of ourselves. We are taught all the important skills needed to survive. We achieve necessary learning in preschool, kindergarten, middle school and high school. Some of us are fortunate enough to attend university, and maybe go on to grad school, and become bankers, consultants, financiers, marketers, scientists, teachers, professors, doctors, librarians, dentists, firemen/women, law enforcement specialists, secretaries, writers, philosophers, inventors, businessmen/women... the list of specialized professionals contributing to society is endless. Our analytical minds have been honed by classroom studies and further enhanced by the practice of a trade.

In a nutshell, it is the Mind that gathers and processes all the information we are exposed to over time, whether in a formal or informal fashion. The Mind thinks based on the data we feed it, which is not ours but is from the outside. The Mind uses all five senses—*sight, smell, hearing, taste,* and *touch* to collect and categorize data, and this data makes impressions on our Mind based upon which we react and act. *A serene Mind does not hold on to impressions*—it observes the data, without reacting to it—this is what it means to be *aware.* I did not believe it to be possible until I witnessed it in my Guru and other enlightened souls, and started living in awareness myself.

Unfulfilled desires make deeper impressions on our Mind and, in turn, make us unhappy. Strong desires make for an even stronger intensity of thoughts, resulting in a powerful impression on the mind. With so many impressions there has to be confusion and indecisiveness. When the Mind is struggling to find a solution it hands the decision making to the intellect. The Mind has the information but our intellect observes and discriminates useful from useless and makes decisions. In other words, the Mind knows but is unable to decide, however, our intellect is able to decide because it can discriminate. Intellect is a refined form of the mind.

With all the information and impressions from formal education (schools and universities) and informal education (parenting, books, TV and movies, radio, internet, etc.) you have reached where you are in life. Has it been enough? Has it made you feel accomplished or happy? Do you feel fulfilled or feel something is missing?

It is probably not enough—because you are still looking for something. Something that will fulfill you. That nameless desire to feed something within you. You still have that place within you which no accomplishment has satisfied. That place which nothing has been fully or permanently able to fulfill.

Strong will and Mind have the ability to fulfill your materialistic goals and needs but they cannot fulfill you, because you are more than the Mind. However, we are used to thinking and associating ourselves with our Mind and its identities with things, which are only on the surface. Attributes like your gender, heritage, nationality, status in society, friends, homes, cars, designer shoes and bags, designer apparel, designer furniture, club affiliations, abilities, family, children and their standing in the society, etc., all those associations can be a source of pride, satisfaction or shame, but not of fulfillment.

You might be thinking this is easier said than done. I agree with you. But nothing is too difficult if there is a desire to do it. It is said, *"A soldier fights a few days in his life, but the battle over Mind goes on day and night for an entire lifetime."* That saying embodies the effort and dedication required to win over your mind. This elusive fulfillment can be achieved whenever you desire, you just need to control your thoughts. It is the nature of the Mind to go after what you do not have. If your desire becomes strong enough, the intensity of your thoughts starts burning a hole in your Mind for peace and happiness and the Mind will become confused and go to the intellect for help and your quest for peace will become priority.

> ***Mind, indeed, is a double edged sword.*** **You must learn to wield it in the direction of your choosing.**

One of the surest ways to begin taking control is to start keeping an eye on your Mind, just like one keeps an eye on an employee. Everyone puts their best foot forward when they are being watched and our Mind is no exception. "What does that really mean," you ask, "to keep an eye on your Mind?" Exactly that—for example, start noticing when you're taking your frustration out on someone else unnecessarily or when you're eating your stress or hurting yourself by worrying. You will notice your thought pattern changing as you observe yourself. At this moment notice your breathing. Is it shallow or deep? Did it get deeper as you paid attention to it? As your breath became deeper, did you notice a smile on your face? Pay attention to your breath and smile all the time.

A few years ago I ran into an unpleasant situation during a trip. I caught a mistake an airline employee made during check-in. He was upset at being caught and proceeded to go on a "power trip" with me. As luck would have it, at the boarding gate I ran into the same individual. He wanted me to check in my carry-on, which was within the permissible size and weight limits, however, he allowed other passengers with bigger bags to board the plane with their carry-ons. My first instinct was to point out the obvious, complain and give him a piece of my mind, but since I was aware of my thoughts I did not do any such thing. Instead I gave him a genuine smile, looked into his eyes and said in a neutral tone, "You must have a reason to check in my bag even though it is within the weight and size limits." He was dumbfounded and did not have an answer. I had not accused him but simply asked for an explanation neutrally, and he did not feel defensive but rather guilty. He said, "Let me check again if your bag will fit in the overhead bin." And then he let me take my bag with me. I thanked him, told him to have a great day and boarded the plane.

It all comes back to the fact that we emote the way we think, and we think the way we emote. It is a vicious circle. If I was not aware of my thoughts, I would have been justifiably angry with the airline employee. But being aware helped me to accept my thoughts, and my emotions did not run with the Mind and helped me behave in a calm fashion and achieve my goal – I got to keep that peace of mind. Our brain changes, adapts and reorganizes neural pathways in response to changes in the environment—as you practice deep breathing and *pranayama* it becomes easier for the new neuropathways to be built. The more aware you become the happier you are because you begin to understand that being happy doesn't mean everything is perfect—rather it is about looking beyond the imperfections.

The Mind plays a major role in our journey towards loving and accepting ourselves, and in turn others, without strings attached. It's akin to writing a new command structure for your existing system as you retrain your Mind to think and act differently. The process of retraining old muscles and creating new connecting pathways in the brain takes patience, will and desire.

Until we practice awareness, attaining freedom from attaching ourselves to the passing thoughts will be difficult. As long as we are attached to our thoughts we are at the mercy of our Mind and making continuous impressions. Think of thoughts as the flow of traffic passing by your window. All kinds of vehicles pass by—small cars, big cars, SUVs, vans, trucks, garbage trucks, semi-trucks, RVs, trucks carrying steel, trucks carrying refrigerated products, trucks carrying hazardous materials, etc.... As you watch these vehicles pass by, you do not stop them or jump into them, even if you see a Lamborghini that you desire. You admire it and let it pass, the same way you would look at the garbage truck passing— you observe not liking its smell and let it pass, and soon the vehicles stop registering in your conscious Mind. Similarly, think of your thoughts as traffic passing by your window, watch them and let them go.

You are experiencing awareness when you can watch the comings and goings of your thoughts without paying attention to them. Soon the thoughts stop coming because they are bored, the Mind begins enjoying the lull, old impressions start fading and inner joy starts taking a deeper foothold.

Over the centuries, in different parts of the world many Saints/Enlightened beings/Gods and Goddesses have been born and worshipped across cultures. I find one Hindu goddess of particular interest. She is depicted as a wild looking female with her hair down, wearing an animal skin around the waist and a red cloth thrown loosely over her shoulders, riding a donkey. She is known as Goddess Kali. I have been fascinated by this Goddess since childhood but never fully understood her until I began my journey inward. Most of the other Hindu female deities are either riding a lion or sitting on a lotus flower in their portrayals, the significance of which I understood as I got older, but I still did not understand the significance of the donkey. I felt that a Goddess should have better clothes and transport, and was further surprised when I learned that she is believed to be one of the most powerful and benevolent Goddesses. I had a hard time wrapping my head around the symbol of her depiction until a few years ago. With the grace of my Guru, my own inner self provided me with an answer.

Goddess Kali's vehicle, the donkey, is depicted as a symbol of the Mind which needs to be conquered and ridden. In old times, before fuel or the wheel was discovered, donkeys were used for manual labor and at the end of the day, when we were done, we tied them to a pole and forgot about them until morning. If only it could be that easy with our Minds. The better control you have over your Mind, the freer you are—that is why Goddess Kali is depicted as wild and free, showing us the way to our own freedom by ruling the Mind.

Unfortunately, most of us are not as free as we have not tamed the donkey/our Mind. Rather our Mind dances to the tune of our five senses and is victim to the six-pronged Mind and often gets corrupted, polluted and addicted as a result of repeated thought patterns—like a beggar with a begging bowl of desires—as soon as one desire is fulfilled another one is standing behind it. After I finished my Master's degree I remember being quite anxious to find an internship. After much effort I found one and was very thankful. Then my next thought was that I hope I get paid. This was a natural thought but until I got the internship (my first desire), I did not care if it was a paid internship or not; but once I had the internship, my next desire to be paid was right behind it. Then I wanted weekends off—my third desire... you get the picture.

The Mind is like computer software for us to use in our daily work. You still need to be in charge and give it commands. Think about the first time you got your computer or tablet. What's the first thing the sales rep told you to do or that maybe you already knew? Install antivirus software of some kind...make sure your firewall is working...block pop-ups...the list goes on. If you have a smart phone then it likely started with a protective case to guard against scratches, nicks, water, shock, etc., followed by super secure apps that are password (or fingerprint) protected. Or maybe you bought a new external hard drive and it came with not only a password but also a hard combination lock too!

We take every step necessary to protect our media devices inside and out. What about the software of our very being? One could argue we do a good job of covering the hardware but have any of us thought twice about the software—i.e. our Mind?

Our Mind needs protection to keep it functioning in a positive way—protection from negative energy, people with negative thinking, negative messaging, repeated patterns of self-sabotage, negative vibrations, and everything that keeps it from functioning the way YOU want it to, the way YOU need it to.

When our dishwasher starts to leave a hazy film on our glasses and china we run the dishwasher with a cycle of vinegar to clean it. At times we even need to use a special dish washing liquid that contains a specific cleanser to keep the dishes sparkling every time. When things go out of gear in life, you cannot put your Mind through a vinegar rinse cycle but you can quiet it with calmness, peace and love.

The Mind likes to be busy until it learns to be still. It likes to keep occupied, so give it an occupation of your choice rather than chaos, one that will help you be at peace. For example, you can ask your Mind to follow your breath and see where it reaches, how far it goes and which part of the body it reaches, without changing your breathing pattern—just by observing.

To begin with try this exercise for 3-5 minutes:

- Close your eyes
- Follow your breath
- Observe the inhalation and follow the air going in from your nose or mouth
- Notice if your chest expands or not
- Notice how the breath feels going in
- Explore the path of the inhalation
- Notice if it feels any different coming out than going in
- Notice the calmness that is descending upon you
- Notice your breaths getting deeper on their own
- See if you can find the boundaries of your thoughts—are they limited to your mind, your physical body? Or do they go beyond it—ponder on this a moment…
- Bring your awareness back to your breathing
- If your mind tries to wander—do not fight it—gently, but firmly, bring it back to the awareness of your breath
- The more you practice the easier it will become for you to bring your mind to the present moment

You are as powerful as your control over
your Mind, and control of breath can
give you that power

Breath and acceptance are the crux of everything and can be thought of as the antivirus for your Mind. As you pay more and more attention to your breathing and practice *pranayama*, you will realize and experience that there is much power in simple breathing and acceptance.

Next time you look at your technology or unplug from your smart phone, take a moment to make sure your own antivirus is also on and stable.

You have to be more Mindful of where you take your Mind. Just like when you are walking on the road and you notice a puddle of dirty water or dog excrement, what do you do? Do you step into the muck or step aside avoiding the muck so that your shoes don't get dirty and there are no splashes on your body or clothes?

I am fairly certain that you step aside keeping yourself, your shoes and clothes clean. Then why not apply the same principle to your thoughts? Your Mind can be your ally and help you discern which landmines to avoid, and walk among your thoughts cleanly until you become the observer and simply let them pass without engaging. All you have to do is make a conscious decision. If you can be Mindful of what you put on your body, and what you eat for your physical body, then you can be Mindful of what impressions you make on your psychic body. You are using the same Mind. The same principles apply.

You programmed your Mind at some time very early in your life to avoid stepping into anything dirty. That is something you observed and learned to do at a relatively young age, perhaps, because your parents or other caretakers taught you. But perhaps no one pointed out that it is more important to have positive impressions by keeping your inner self clean. This is a secret very few know, and one can teach only what one knows.

It is like cleaning a peanut butter or mayonnaise jar. How do you clean it? You may put the jar in the dishwasher—hot, soapy water is squirted in it a few times to get the sticky product off the sides of the jar; then clean water is squirted in and then it is dried with hot air. However, the jar may still not be clean after one wash cycle, depending on how clean the jar was to begin with, if it was rinsed or not beforehand. I usually put warm water and a drop of dishwater liquid in the jar, shake it nicely and leave it for a minute or two, then dump the muck. I usually have to do this more than once for peanut butter jars, even if I am just cleaning it to recycle the jar.

Breathing does the same thing for our nerves. You take a nice, deep breath, and with your inhalation that life force energy cleans and rejuvenates your nerves.

The exhale is equally important and does far more than just get rid of carbon dioxide from our lungs. A deeper exhale pulls the sludge of negative energy out of the whole body.

Try this exercise. Now that your Mind knows the importance, it will help you and guide you. Close your eyes, and

- Take a deep breath—as you breathe in visualize the life force energy going in your body and spreading everywhere from head to toe
- Hold your inhale for a few seconds and enjoy

this sensation of fullness

- Exhale and visualize as you press your stomach muscles against your ribs that as your lungs are releasing CO_2, your body/nerves are releasing toxins and they are leaving your body in each exhale
- Hold your exhale—even for a second—and savor this empty feeling. Then start the cycle of breathing again. Inhale—hold—Exhale—hold

Please stop and repeat this breathing exercise with Mind, your friend. Allow it to guide you and help you. Do this 3 to 4 times, and notice how you feel.

Now that you know how to sidestep negativity by choosing not to react to any given situation by stepping aside and taking a deep breath or two, you have taken charge of your Mind. You have chosen to command rather than be led by your Mind. By doing so you gain control over your emotions which means:

- You feel more positive and happier
- You feel more and more in charge of the circumstances around you
- You are more focused and can get more done in the same amount of time
- Your energy stays higher for longer periods of time and makes you more efficient
- Your blood pressure stays in the normal range and you get to enjoy a longer healthy life
- You have more patience and acceptance, resulting in better interpersonal relations

At this point you probably have a smile on your face. You are feeling kind of empty, yet full. Your Mind is at rest and at peace, and thankful to be resting. Now enjoy this feeling and remember you can create it anytime, anywhere. YOU are the BOSS.

The more aware you are of your breath, the more control you will have of your Mind. The more control you have of your Mind, the more acceptance you will have of where you are in life. The more acceptance you have, the more love you will have for yourself. The more love and acceptance you have of self, the more acceptance and love you will have for others. Love and acceptance leads to flow of positive energy, and that gives you the ability to soar like a hawk and walk like an elephant, and your vibrations are harmonious and you enjoy better health and relations, and are more creative, successful and content—and your Mind is serene and calm like a water body with no waves.

> *"I will not let anyone walk through my Mind with their dirty feet."* ~ Mahatma Gandhi

Epilogue

So, will you let your mind be a beggar?

Acknowledgements

My family, friends and students have been telling me for a long time to write a book so that this information reaches many more than only those in my close proximity. I resisted writing this book for quite some time because I knew how involved the process would be, as I had watched my father write and publish books multiple times. One day the decision was out of my hands, my Guru decided for me. Since the inspiration came from him, writing the content of *Mind, the Beggar?* became the easy part.

My Guru's grace is such that he provided two wonderful people to bring about the manifestation of this book into physical form - Shruti and Surbhi transformed my hand written notes into what you have read. If it was not for their commitment and dedication to the project, their persistent focus and countless edits and re-edits, you and I would not have had the pleasure of holding this book in our hands

My special thanks to my husband without whom I would not have been successful on this journey. His patience, understanding and sacrifices are big blessings.

I am thankful for Brent's friendship and loving hands to usher this book through the final phases of publication. I am grateful for his continuous thoughtfulness, kindness and belief in the project.

There are many more people who were instrumental in bringing this project to fruition that are not mentioned here individually, but whom I treasure and thank for their expertise, support, friendship and love.

I am, and will forever be, thankful to all of you.

Thoughts from Readers

I hope there is something here for everyone, and that it helps you as much as it has helped those I have encountered on this journey. Below are some thoughts from those who have travelled or are travelling on this path today:

"Despite the affluence in which most people live in the Western world, it seems that happiness is still woefully out of reach. Mind, the Beggar? *uncovers universal truths and tools to living a happy, fulfilling life—every day. The book opened my eyes to the reality that my pursuit of happiness was making me miserable. Like a dog chasing its tail, I was never going to catch happiness and, in the process, was making myself mentally and physically sick. We all know to "Stop and smell the roses." But I would guess that most of us rarely take the time to do so. And even when we do—are we actually in the moment and savoring the experience? This small but mighty tome inspired and empowered me to focus inward to tap the source of true happiness and to use the tools it describes to engage my mind, heart and body in manifesting love, acceptance and happiness in my everyday life. Now, instead of putting on a smiling veneer to mask my inner turmoil, I find myself smiling genuinely from an inner core of love and acceptance for both myself and others. The daily practice and consistent focus cost nothing but the returns are immediate and nothing short of phenomenal!"*

~ Former Healthcare consultant

"It is very easy to get sucked into day-to-day life doing things which you don't like, spending [an] entire career working for others and making them rich at the expense of your own family. By the time one realizes that it is too late—children have grown up and have left the home, body starts to frail, all kinds of ailments start to show up and a lot of regrets pop up. All of this can be avoided by having a balanced life, full of vigor, happiness, health and prosperity by following a few simple rules and practices. No matter at what stage of your life you are at the tools in this book will change you forever and for the better. Following these techniques has done wonders for me resulting in a much happier, healthier and thankful individual with a positive look towards all aspects of life."

~ Senior Executive in the Chemicals industry

"I've always had a plan. When I was 18 it was a college degree in engineering and COO job one day. At 22 it was consulting then COO. When I was 25 it was partner by 30, then a family (and maybe still COO). Now at 30 let's just say my plans haven't worked out as I thought they would. I've finally stopped making plans and what I've learned from my guru over the last few years as I've dealt with my plans crashing around me, I wish I knew a long time ago. Some of what you'll read today may seem simplistic but when followed with faith it works. I was a skeptical student from the beginning but nothing else I had tried worked for me so I went with it and am thankful every day. I hope something helps you on your journey, sooner rather than later."

~ Management Consultant and Operations expert

"*I have often felt dualistic in terms of worldly and spiritual, and my life journey in the past few years has augmented that feeling. I struggled with how to balance the drive to succeed on a worldly level and the desire to continue on the spiritual path, which seem contradictory on the surface.*

This book has changed my outlook and approach towards life. It has helped me understand that being worldly or spiritual is not mutually exclusive. This acceptance of my current state and desires has helped me grow as a person."

~ Financial Analyst at Fortune 500 company

About the Author

Anandmai was born and raised in India. Throughout her adult life she has had multiple opportunities to live, work, study, teach and raise a family in Ireland, the United States and India. She has been blessed with life experiences that have ranged from poverty to abundance and despair to inner resolve, love, acceptance and lasting happiness. Her greatest blessings have been her family and spiritual teachers. Anandmai currently lives in the Chicagoland area and continues to share and teach the universal, spiritual truths and wisdom she came to know through her spiritual journey.

www.ingramcontent.com/pod-product-compliance
Lightning Source LLC
Chambersburg PA
CBHW060514030426
42337CB00015B/1882